POLLY TEALE

Polly Teale is the Joint Artistic Director of Shared Experience Theatre Company. *Brontë* is the third and final play to explore the work and world of the Brontë family, following on from her adaptation of *Jane Eyre* and her original play, *After Mrs Rochester*, which was based on the life of Jean Rhys and her novel *Wide Sargasso Sea*, itself inspired by *Jane Eyre*.

In addition to directing the premiere productions of these three plays for Shared Experience – and winning the Evening Standard Best Director Award for *After Mrs Rochester* – Polly's work for the company includes directing *The Clearing*, *A Doll's House*, *The House of Bernarda Alba*, *Desire under the Elms*, *Madame Bovary: Breakfast with Emma* and co-directing *War and Peace* and *The Mill on the Floss* with Nancy Meckler.

Her other directing credits include *Angels and Saints* for Soho Theatre; *The Glass Menagerie* at the Lyceum, Edinburgh; *Miss Julie* at the Young Vic; *Babies* and *Uganda* at the Royal Court; *A Taste of Honey* for English Touring Theatre; *Somewhere* at the National Theatre; *Waiting at the Water's Edge* at The Bush Theatre; *What Is Seized* at the Drill Hall; and *Ladies in the Lift* at Soho Poly.

Polly's writing credits also include *Afters* for BBC Screen Two and *Fallen* for the Traverse Theatre, Edinburgh.

Other Titles in this Series

AFTER MRS ROCHESTER
Polly Teale
Based on the life and work of
  Jean Rhys

ANIMAL FARM
Ian Wooldridge
Adapted from George Orwell

ANNA KARENINA
Helen Edmundson
Adapted from Leo Tolstoy

ARABIAN NIGHTS
Dominic Cooke

BEAUTY AND THE BEAST
Laurence Boswell

CINDERELLA
Stuart Paterson

CORAM BOY
Helen Edmundson
Adapted from Jamila Gavin

DR JEKYLL AND MR
HYDE
David Edgar
Adapted from
  Robert Louis Stevenson

EMMA
Martin Millar
  & Doon MacKichan
Adapted from Jane Austen

GONE TO EARTH
Helen Edmundson
Adapted from Mary Webb

HANSEL AND GRETEL
Stuart Paterson

HIS DARK MATERIALS
Nicholas Wright
Adapted from Philip Pullman

JANE EYRE
Polly Teale
Adapted from
  Charlotte Brontë

KES
Lawrence Till
Adapted from Barry Hines

MADAME BOVARY
Fay Weldon
Adapted from
  Gustave Flaubert

THE MILL ON THE FLOSS
Helen Edmundson
Adapted from George Eliot

MISERYGUTS
  & TARTUFFE
Liz Lochhead
Adapted from Molière

NORTHANGER ABBEY
Tim Luscombe
Adapted from Jane Austen

SLEEPING BEAUTY
Rufus Norris

SUNSET SONG
Alastair Cording
Adapted from
  Lewis Grassic Gibbon

WAR AND PEACE
Helen Edmundson
Adapted from Leo Tolstoy

Polly Teale

BRONTË

NICK HERN BOOKS
London
www.nickhernbooks.co.uk

A Nick Hern Book

Brontë first published in Great Britain as a paperback original
in 2005 by Nick Hern Books Limited, 14 Larden Road,
London W3 7ST

Brontë copyright © 2005 Polly Teale

Cover image: Mark Pennington

Typeset by Country Setting, Kingsdown, Kent CT14 8ES
Printed in Great Britain by Bookmarque, Croydon, Surrey

A CIP catalogue record for this book is available from
the British Library

ISBN-13   978 1 85459 882 0
ISBN-10   1 85459 882 1

Introduction

In 1837, the poet Robert Southey wrote to the young Charlotte
Brontë, who had confided in him her literary ambitions:
' . . . the daydreams in which you indulge are likely to produce
a distempered state of mind . . . Literature cannot be the
business of a woman's life and ought not to be. The more she
is engaged in her proper duties, the less time she will have for
it, even as a recreation.' Charlotte replied: 'Sir, I cannot rest
until I have answered your letter. I felt only shame and regret
that I had ventured to trouble you . . . a painful heat rose to my
face when I thought of the quires of paper I had covered with
what once gave me so much delight but which was now only a
source of confusion . . . I trust I shall never more feel ambitious
to see my name in print. If the wish should arise I'll look to
Southey's letter and suppress it.' There is no evidence that she
wrote anything for the next two years.

Today it is difficult for us to imagine a world where women
were not allowed to enter a library, where women had to publ
under men's names, where women had no part in public lif
And yet 150 years is not so long ago. Their struggles are r
distant. We are fascinated by the Brontës because they br
the mould (against all odds). They broke it and yet they
made by it. They were every inch the product of their ti
even in their attempts to free themselves. *Jane Eyre* is l
to be the second-most read book in the English langua
the Bible). *Wuthering Heights* remains one of the gre
creations of all time and is still a bestseller. So why,
later, are we still so drawn to these stories, these ch

In 1997, I adapted *Jane Eyre* for Shared Experienc
company, we are interested in theatre's potential to
what is hidden, to give form to the world of imagir
and memory, to go beyond the surface of every
what literature can do so powerfully: when we
novel we are allowed to enter the consciousne
ters, to know their most intimate fears and lo

world as if through their eyes. *Jane Eyre* is exactly such a creation. Everything in the novel is seen through the magnifying glass of Jane's psyche. But if this is a psychological drama with Jane at its centre, why did Brontë invent a mad woman, Bertha, Rochester's first wife, locked in an attic to torment her heroine? Why is this rational young woman haunted by a raving, vengeful she-devil? I (along with many others, including the artist Paula Rego, who has painted a whole series of work inspired by *Jane Eyre*) was intrigued by the mythic power of the mad woman, by Charlotte Brontë's repulsion and attraction to her creation, by the mad woman's danger and eroticism, her terrifying rage. I wanted to explore what she represented, how she came into existence, to understand how the mad woman had been born in reaction to the Victorian ideal of femininity, how she had grown out of the Victorian consciousness.

Later, I went on to write a play – *After Mrs Rochester* – about Jean Rhys, whose novel, *Wide Sargasso Sea*, is a prequel to *Jane Eyre*, imagining the mad woman's life before she was locked away, giving the first Mrs Rochester her own story. Here the mad woman is no longer a monster. We discover her as a child, follow her journey, her growing alienation, knowing where it will end. *Wide Sargasso Sea* became a modern classic. The mad woman was out of her attic, back on the run, ready to stray into our fiction in whatever form she might choose, a symbol of female power and psychosis.

Brontë is my third and final play on this subject. As the title suggests, it marks a return to the source, to the beginning: the Brontës themselves. How was it possible that these women, three celibate Victorian sisters, living in isolation on the Yorkshire moors, could have written some of the most passionate (even erotic) fiction of all time? Perhaps the simplest answer lies in their father (their mother died when they were children). Self-educated, from illiterate Irish peasant stock, he went on to Cambridge and later published books of his own poems and sermons. He was a passionate believer in the transformative power of literature and art. He educated his daughters and encouraged them to read whatever they could lay their hands on (most women at the time would have had carefully supervised reading). The Brontës read Byron, Shakespeare, George Sand, Milton and Shelley. From childhood they wrote

books (on tiny pages made out of old flour and sugar bags), not knowing this was out of the ordinary, not yet knowing what was and wasn't allowed. But soon the sisters faced harsh reality. Highly educated, intelligent, full of curiosity and hunger for life, they entered a world with little or no place for them. As poor, plain women their life prospects were severely limited. Becoming a governess was virtually the only profession available to them. The sisters' attempts to work as governesses were lonely and short-lived. Anne was the only one who managed to hold down a job for more than a few months. It was never long before they returned home.

Their responses to their predicament were complex and individual: Emily refused to wear a corset or petticoats and withdrew from society, spending much of her time alone on the moors; Charlotte was hugely ambitious, longing for fame and recognition; Anne, the youngest, developed a strong social perspective, writing to expose injustice and bring about reform. Emily and Charlotte's reactions to their isolation could not have been more different. It took Charlotte months to persuade Emily to consider publishing her work; for Emily, writing was a deeply private act, her invisibility a cloak that allowed her to live as a recluse, in communion with nature, untouched by social constraints or expectations. She never forgave Charlotte for betraying her real identity to her publisher by letting slip that the author was in fact a woman.

Meanwhile, their brother Branwell, floundering under the weight of the family's impossibly high expectations, returned home heavily in debt, an alcoholic and a drug addict. The Brontës were once again living under the same roof, back in the intimate proximity of childhood. It was through Branwell that the sisters experienced the horror of mental illness as he descended into paranoia, bringing chaos to the household. It was also Branwell who provided the source of their sexual knowledge: caught up in a series of affairs, he allowed the sisters to share vicariously in his adventures.

All three sisters used their brother as a model for their fictional characters. He appears in various guises in their work according to their relationship with him. Charlotte, who was closest to Branwell as a child, later became the most estranged. Her outrage at his degenerate behaviour was in part a way of dealing with her own bitter frustrations. Lonely and unloved, she was forced to look on as her brother satisfied his appetites.

Here we return to the mad woman, perhaps the most sexual of all the Brontë creations, and the question of where she came from, what she represented. She is both a hideous monster and an exotic temptress, raised to enchant, to seduce. Rochester's description of her when they first met in the West Indies is irresistible. She is Charlotte's fantasy of herself, beautiful and desired. She comes from the land of the Brontë's imagination, from a land of hot rain and hurricanes. She is both dangerous and exciting. She is passionate and sexual, angry and violent. She is the embodiment of everything that Charlotte feared in herself and longed to express, of everything Charlotte's life could never be.

'I can hardly tell you how life gets on here at Haworth. There is not an event whatever to mark its progress. One day resembles another and all have lifeless physiognomies. Sunday, baking day, and Saturday are the only ones that bear the slightest distinctive mark. Meantime, time wears away. I shall soon be 30 and I have done nothing yet . . . I feel as if we were all buried here. I long to travel, to work, to live a life of action.'

Although Charlotte would never 'live a life of action' in the external, physical sense, she would travel the world in her imagination. The external lives of the Brontë sisters were dreary, repetitive, uneventful, and yet their inner lives were the opposite. To tell this story we need to dramatise the collision between drab domesticity and unfettered, soaring imagination, to see both the real and internal world, at once, to make visible what is hidden inside. That is why in our play the characters from the novels are living in the house, haunting their creators. While the sisters cook and clean and sew there exists another world full of passion and fury. It seems to me that the theatre is the right place to tell this particular tale. After all, this is a story of make-believe, of the power of the imagination to transcend time and place and circumstance, to take us to places we cannot otherwise go.

Polly Teale

This article first appeared in The Guardian, *13 August 2005*

For Ian and Eden

Brontë was first performed by Shared Experience Theatre Company at the Yvonne Arnaud Theatre, Guildford, on 25 August 2005, and subsequently at West Yorkshire Playhouse, Leeds; Warwick Arts Centre; Project Arts Centre, Dublin; York Theatre Royal; Oxford Playhouse; Liverpool Playhouse; the Lyric Hammersmith, London; and The Lowry, Salford. The cast was as follows:

CHARLOTTE	Fenella Woolgar
EMILY	Diane Beck
ANNE	Catherine Cusack
BERTHA/CATHY	Natalia Tena
BRANWELL/ARTHUR HUNTINGDON & HEATHCLIFF	Matthew Thomas
PATRICK/BELL NICHOLLS/ ROCHESTER & MR HEGER	David Fielder

All other characters played by members of the company

Director   Polly Teale
Designer   Angela Davies
Featuring images by   Paula Rego
Composer and Sound Designer   Peter Salem
Movement Director   Leah Hausman
Lighting Designer   Chris Davey

10

Author's Note

The play begins with a Prologue during which the actors change from modern dress into Victorian costumes. As they change, they shift into character taking on Yorkshire accents.

The present tense of the first half of the play takes place in July 1845, the day when Anne and Branwell return from Thorpe Green where they have been working as governess and tutor. At this time Emily was writing *Wuthering Heights* and Charlotte about to write *Jane Eyre*. Hence the presence of Cathy (the heroine from *Wuthering Heights*) and Bertha (the mad woman from *Jane Eyre*).

Cathy and Bertha appear on stage as they surface in the minds of their creators. Emily is writing the section of *Wuthering Heights* where Cathy is feverish and delirious, close to the end of her life. She has torn open her pillow and is obsessively trying to remember the names of the birds from which the feathers come, in the belief that it will reconnect her to her childhood, to the free, primitive self. The image of Cathy unable to recognise her reflection, unable to recognise her adult self in the mirror is central to both Cathy's and Emily's crisis. Their fear of being neutered, being destroyed by conformity. Whenever Cathy and Nelly (her maid, given voice by Emily) or Cathy and Emily are indicated as speaking together, they should not speak in exact unison but as if Emily were hearing Cathy's voice as she writes. Cathy speaks with a Yorkshire accent.

Bertha first surfaces in Charlotte's childhood fantasy of herself as the beautiful daughter, admired by all. Later Bertha, the mad woman, becomes an expression of the part of Charlotte (sexual longing, rage, frustration, loneliness) which she wishes to disown, to conceal from others. In the second half of the play, when *Jane Eyre* comes to life, Charlotte takes on the role of Jane, casting herself as the 'good angel', the moral centre of the story and antithesis of Bertha. I have included some stage

directions to suggest Bertha's physical presence on stage.
Whenever she appears, she expresses the feeling that Charlotte
is trying to suppress. Charlotte should be physically affected
by Bertha's movements (even as she struggles to conceal it) so
we understand that Bertha is a manifestation of Charlotte's
inner life. Bertha speaks with a West Indian accent.

The rest of the first half is a series of flashbacks which
progress through the Brontës' childhood returning to July 1845
towards the end of the act.

A dash (–) indicates that the speaker is interrupted at that point.
An ellipsis (. . .) indicates that the speech trails off.

Polly Teale

Thanks to Angela Simpson, RADA, English Touring Theatre,
Anna at Stagetext, the staff of the British Library, *Brontë*
workshop participants – Helen Schlesinger, Monica Dolan,
Penny Layden, Sarah Ball, Hannah Miles, Richard Atlee,
Jay Villiers, James Clyde and Nafeesah Butt – and the Brontë
biographers, without whom this play could never have been
written.

Special thanks to Anne Dinsdale, Librarian at the Brontë
Parsonage Museum, for answering endless questions and being
an invaluable resource.

Characters

THE BRONTË FAMILY

PATRICK
CHARLOTTE
BRANWELL
EMILY
ANNE

THE GHOSTS, *both played by the same person*

CATHERINE EARNSHAW (CATHY),
  from Wuthering Heights
BERTHA MASON, *from* Jane Eyre

The actor playing Patrick also plays

ROCHESTER, *from* Jane Eyre
ARTHUR BELL NICHOLLS, *Patrick's curate*
MR HEGER, *Charlotte's tutor*

The actor playing Branwell also plays

HEATHCLIFF, *from* Wuthering Heights
ARTHUR HUNTINGTON, *from* The Tenant of Wildfell Hall

ACT ONE

The stage suggests the interior of the Brontë parsonage. The back rooms of the house are marked out on the floor with gaffer tape. There is a kitchen table and three chairs. The walls rise up into a vast stormy sky. Scattered about the stage there are books both old and new.

The actors playing the three sisters change out of modern clothes and into costume during the Prologue.

The women address the audience.

EMILY. How did it happen?

ANNE. How was it possible?

CHARLOTTE. Three Victorian spinsters living in isolation on the Yorkshire moors.

ANNE. There are books. There are people who have spent months, years, half a lifetime

CHARLOTTE. examining every scrap, every scribbled note. The doodle in the margin.

EMILY. Their house is a museum. Every year thousands of people walk around it, staring at their underwear, their darned stockings, a rotting corset.

ANNE. Peering at the tiny books they wrote as children, made out of old flour and sugar bags cut up and sewn together, filled with writing too small to read.

CHARLOTTE. There have been endless films, documentaries, dramas.

ANNE. They who were so quiet in life. Living unseen.

CHARLOTTE. Unnoticed.

EMILY. Invisible.

CHARLOTTE. They have become celebrities in death.

ANNE. They were not pretty.

EMILY. Or fashionable.

CHARLOTTE. There was no scandal.

ANNE. They never drank alcohol or took drugs.

CHARLOTTE. They had never had sex.

ANNE. They were probably never even kissed. (*Tries to imagine this.*)

EMILY. But they wrote some of the most passionate literature of all time.

CHARLOTTE. They, with their plain faces. They, who'd never aroused another human being in the flesh. Who'd never touched, tasted, smelt, felt –

EMILY. fucked –

ANNE. have aroused so many in their absence. (*Beat.*) How did they do it? (*Beat.*) How did they know?

Beat.

CHARLOTTE. We try to imagine, try to picture them.

EMILY. It's hard to believe that they really dressed like this (*Looking down at the dress she is putting on.*) for walking on the moors, carrying in coal, scrubbing floors.

ANNE. Writing books!

CHARLOTTE. There's the painting done by their brother Branwell, now hanging in the National Portrait Gallery.

BRANWELL *enters carrying a Brontë biography.* CHARLOTTE *takes it from him and looks at the cover on which is* BRANWELL*'s painting of the sisters.*

There is a smudge in the middle where he has painted himself out. (*Indicating* CHARLOTTE*'s portrait.*) She looks too fat.

ANNE. Too miserable.

EMILY. Too pinched.

CHARLOTTE. Not that they were pretty. Not at all. Never. Not once was that word used.

ANNE. Their lives would have been different if they had been. They would have married.

EMILY. Died in childbirth.

CHARLOTTE. Or had lots of children and never written another word.

ANNE. Perhaps the odd recipe, a letter here and there, but nothing *you* (*To the audience.*) would know about.

CHARLOTTE. They would be gone.

ANNE. Lost.

CHARLOTTE. Sunk without trace.

EMILY. In the deep dark river that claims us all.

Beat.

ANNE. We have no mother. Can none of us remember her. That's why our books are peopled by orphans. Children abandoned.

EMILY. Lost.

CHARLOTTE. Alone.

ANNE. We cannot imagine what it would have been like to have kisses and cuddles. A woman's soft touch. Her warmth and forgiveness.

CHARLOTTE. Perhaps that is why we're so uncommonly close. So uneasy with strangers.

ANNE. Perhaps that is why we have little patience with children. Why we are utterly ill-suited to the only job available to us.

ALL. Governess.

ANNE. There are stories about our mother, things we've been told. A bird was once trapped in the house. It flew again and again at the window. Broke its wing, its beak, its leg. She kept it and nursed it back to life.

CHARLOTTE. She used to make up tales of foreign lands at bedtime.

ANNE. Broke its wing, its beak, its leg. She kept it and nursed it back to life.

CHARLOTTE. No mother. Can't remember. Not a word, not a look, not a smile.

EMILY. We were lucky.

CHARLOTTE. Lucky?

ANNE. How so?

EMILY. She was not there to criticise. To insist on ladylike manners, pretty clothes and gentle speech. To organise tea parties with eligible men. We were allowed to read whatever we found. Whatever we could get hold of.

The actor playing PATRICK BRONTË *brings a pile of books and places them on the table.* CHARLOTTE, EMILY *and* ANNE *read the spines eagerly.*

Milton. Byron. Shelley.

CHARLOTTE. Scott. Homer. Shakespeare. Brontë. Patrick Brontë . . . Yes. (*Pause.*) Our name printed on the spine in beautiful curling letters.

ANNE. Our father, born Brunty, an Irish peasant, had himself published, at some expense, a volume of poems and a book of sermons that sit alongside the rest.

PATRICK. The word. It is this alone which separates us from animals. The power not only to live but to *know* that we are living. That is to think. To shape ourselves. To make of our lives what we would. To inspire others with what we say, what we believe. Look to God, to the great men of history, Look to art, to literature.

ANNE (*looking through the pile of books*). Horace, Bunyan, Johnson –

CHARLOTTE. Thackeray. William Makepeace Thackeray.

EMILY. It did not occur to us that these books were written by men. Not yet.

ANNE. We did not know that we too would be remembered. We could never have imagined, never have dreamed –

CHARLOTTE. Or perhaps I could. Perhaps I was always waiting. Preparing. The thousands of pages covered with words. The letters, the diaries, the books. Who were they for if not for you. (*To the audience.*) You who know me better than any who ever saw my face.

ANNE. I am not so interesting to you. Or only as a sister. My books will be read as background to their great works. While *they* plunder the imagination, that secret, inner world, *I* write about the world that I see . . . and hope, hope to change it a little.

EMILY. You are fascinated by me but I am the hardest to find out about. My book is like a chained door that will only give enough to let you glimpse inside and wonder what it might be like to enter. There are no letters. No diary. My sister Charlotte, after my death, rewrote my poems and burned my second novel.

CHARLOTTE. We don't know that for certain.

EMILY. I had been writing all that summer. There are letters from my publisher urging me not to hurry the ending.

CHARLOTTE. It is not proven.

EMILY. It was written.

CHARLOTTE (*suddenly angry*). Emily. Do you know what they said about you? Can you imagine what it was like?

Beat. CHARLOTTE *and* EMILY *stare at one another.*

Our home, the parsonage, came with the job. If our father were to lose it, we would be homeless. Where would we go?

ANNE. Who would we be?

EMILY. We cannot imagine. This house. This place. This is our world.

ANNE. The events you will see tonight belie the truth. The life we lead would be dull to watch. The cleaning and cooking, the mending and making. Each day the same as the day before.

CHARLOTTE. On the floor is marked out the size and shape of our kitchen.

CHARLOTTE *walks along the gaffer tape that delineates the kitchen.*

EMILY. Our books are covered in flour and spatters of gravy. The library have complained.

CHARLOTTE. Not to us. We are not allowed to go there. Fathers and sons only.

EMILY. But our brother tells us that a carrot peeling was found, lying like a bookmark, by the librarian.

CHARLOTTE. Upstairs, Branwell has his own study. We three girls sleep together.

ANNE. There is a tiny room at the top of the stairs, little more than a cupboard, which Emily has made her own.

CHARLOTTE. That is to say that although there is no lock on the door, we do not go in there, ever.

ANNE. Immediately in front of the house lies the graveyard, the church and then the town. Five thousand inhabitants working mostly in the textile mills in the valley below. Sanitary conditions are poor. Nearly half of all children die before their sixth birthday. The average age of death for a labourer, just twenty-six. Our father is kept very busy.

PATRICK *is heard conducting the funeral service.*

PATRICK. Man that is born of woman has but a short time to live . . . *etc.*

He continues on under the following lines.

EMILY. Some days there are four, five people buried.

CHARLOTTE. Among them our mother and two older sisters.

ANNE. I run my fingers over the letters on the gravestone.

EMILY. You can hear the sound of shovels from our house. And Father's voice. He knows these words by heart as do most of his congregation.

CHARLOTTE. Few people can read. Even fewer write.

Beat.

EMILY. Beyond the house is the moor.

EMILY *stands, wearing an apron, looking out from the back door (towards the audience) as if at the moors. Her sisters come and stand behind her in the doorway.*

CHARLOTTE. The blackened heath.

ANNE. An occasional rock.

EMILY. A low wall that wanders and peters out. Even the path has nowhere to go. Except over the hill, into the sky.

She looks up above the audience's heads. She quotes from Wuthering Heights.

You can guess the power of the north wind by the excessive slant of a few gaunt thorns all stretching their limbs one way, as if craving alms of the sun. As if craving alms of the sun.

A July day in 1845. EMILY *whistles, fingers in mouth, to her hawk. The sisters leave. The hawk swoops down and settles on her arm. She strokes his head a moment, feeds him a scrap of meat, and then releases him, watching him climb high into the sky. At the moment of release* CATHY *appears in her nightgown. She is carrying her pillow and holding a feather up to the light.* EMILY *wipes her hands on her apron and returns to the kitchen table. She is kneading bread. In front of her is a pile of pages and a pen. The unfinished manuscript of* Wuthering Heights. *As she kneads she is reading back to herself the last page of her writing. She has her pencil behind her ear. She corrects the occasional word.* CATHY *speaks the names of the birds with* EMILY.

EMILY. That's a turkey's. And this is a wild duck's, and this a pigeon's. And this, I should know it amongst a thousand.

CATHY. And this, I should know it amongst a thousand. This feather was picked from the heath. It is a lapwing's. Beautiful bird. Wheeling over our heads in the middle of the moor. Riding the wind. Higher and higher.

EMILY. Riding the wind. Higher and higher. Beautiful bird.

CATHY. Beautiful bird. Wheeling over our heads in the middle of the moor. Riding the wind. Higher and higher. Making us run.

EMILY *hears* CHARLOTTE *enter through the front door.*

CHARLOTTE. We need to make up the bed and the fire in Branwell's room. He and Anne are to be home tonight. They sent for the gig yesterday. We must buy some meat, and tobacco and . . . They must have been given leave. He is on his way and will be with us before nightfall. They are coming home.

EMILY. I know.

CHARLOTTE. You know?

EMILY. Anne wrote to me two days ago.

CHARLOTTE. Why did you not tell me?

EMILY. I had thought to tell you today.

CHARLOTTE. Today! Why today? Why not two days ago so that we might make them welcome. We have nothing in the house.

EMILY. I did not want to worry you.

CHARLOTTE. Worry me! You shall worry me when you do not tell me until it is too late to prepare a decent meal or air their beds.

EMILY. The beds are made and soup prepared for supper.

CHARLOTTE. Why didn't you tell me?

EMILY. Because. Because I didn't want to alarm you. Not until it is known what has . . .

CHARLOTTE. What?

EMILY. There is some story. I do not yet know the details.

CHARLOTTE. A story. What story?

EMILY. He is dismissed, and Anne has given notice. They will not return.

CHARLOTTE. What has he done?

EMILY. We will find out tonight.

CHARLOTTE. But you know. She told you in the letter.

EMILY. The baldest of accounts. She says that he is not well.
That he has got himself into trouble.

CHARLOTTE. What kind of trouble?

EMILY. I have told you I know only the –

CHARLOTTE. Tell me.

EMILY. He has had some kind of affair with the mistress of
the house. He is drinking again . . .

CHARLOTTE. Show me the letter.

EMILY. There's no need.

CHARLOTTE. Let me see it.

EMILY. It's not to hand.

CHARLOTTE. Then go and get it.

EMILY. She asked me to keep it to myself.

Silence.

CHARLOTTE *puts on her apron and goes out the kitchen
door into the yard. She returns with the coal scuttle and
begins to put coal into the range.*

CHARLOTTE. Does Father know?

EMILY. I told him just now. That they are coming home but
not the reason why.

CHARLOTTE. So everyone knows but me and I am to be told
at the post office.

EMILY. I was going to tell you as soon as you came –

CHARLOTTE. Soup! We can't give them soup. They have
been travelling all day. We must make it a welcome
whatever the circumstances. I shall go myself to the
butcher's. We shall eat in the dining room. We shall get out
the china, and a plum pudding –

EMILY. They're for Christmas.

CHARLOTTE. We have two.

EMILY. I don't think we should make a fuss.

CHARLOTTE. Fuss! Fuss! Is it a fuss to cook a decent meal?

EMILY. Do as you wish.

CHARLOTTE. I shall.

> CHARLOTTE *sees on the chair an opened parcel. A collection of poetry written by the three sisters under male aliases.*

They sent our poems back.

EMILY. This morning.

CHARLOTTE. What did they say?

EMILY. As ever.

> CHARLOTTE *picks up the letter and reads it. She screws it up.*

CHARLOTTE. We shall send them to another publisher.

EMILY. That was the last one on the list.

CHARLOTTE. Then we shall write another list.

EMILY. Not for me.

CHARLOTTE. What do you mean?

EMILY. I'm going out.

CHARLOTTE. It's about to rain.

EMILY. So I see.

> EMILY *takes off her apron and puts on her boots and shawl during the following.*

CHARLOTTE. Has Father had his medicine?

EMILY. An hour ago.

CHARLOTTE. And you have read to him? The paper looks untouched.

EMILY. He said he was too tired.

CHARLOTTE. You should read to him anyway.

EMILY. To what purpose?

CHARLOTTE. To keep him in the world. It is not good for him to be left alone all day in his own silence.

EMILY. It is his choice.

CHARLOTTE. The less he can see, the more it is for us to keep him with us. He should not be left with only his thoughts, to slip into darkness.

EMILY. I'll be back before supper.

CHARLOTTE. They forecast a storm.

EMILY. I know.

CHARLOTTE. Has Father had his midday tea?

EMILY. It's half past twelve.

CHARLOTTE. I know the time.

EMILY. Then he has had it.

CHARLOTTE. And his drops?

EMILY. They are in the cupboard. They are due in half an hour.

CHARLOTTE. I know.

EMILY. We managed for a year without you.

EMILY *picks up the dog lead and the manuscript of* Wuthering Heights.

EMILY *whistles to her dog.* CHARLOTTE *wipes the table.*

CHARLOTTE. It was not my choice to go away. I didn't choose to spend my every moment with a spoilt child and a miserable baby. To be ordered about 'til I was dead on my feet, day after day. I did it for you. That you might be here and not parted from what you must have.

EMILY. Then let me go to it.

The door opens and PATRICK *stands in the doorway. He has only a little sight left and has used a stick to navigate the journey to the kitchen.*

PATRICK. Why are there voices raised in my kitchen?

CHARLOTTE. Father. You should have rung. You should not –

PATRICK. I should. I should not. It is not for you to tell me what I should or should not do. I should not have had to leave my chair if it wasn't for your quarrel. What is it about?

CHARLOTTE. We were . . . in disagreement over what to cook for dinner. (*Pause.*) Emily has made soup but I would rather –

PATRICK (*to* CHARLOTTE). Go and lay a fire in my study.

CHARLOTTE *leaves.* EMILY *stands, still dressed in her shawl and holding the manuscript of* Wuthering Heights. PATRICK *reaches out and touches the manuscript.*

What are you reading?

EMILY. A book.

PATRICK. Is it good?

EMILY. I . . . don't know. I have not yet finished it.

PATRICK. But you must have an opinion.

EMILY. It is . . . unusual.

PATRICK. Unusual. I am intrigued.

EMILY. It is not so very interesting . . .

PATRICK. Read it to me.

EMILY. It would not be to your taste.

PATRICK. How do you know? (*Pause.*) Wherever you open it. The next sentence. What is it?

EMILY *reads with* CATHY *repeating the words as she pulls feathers from her pillow.*

EMILY. That's a pigeon's –

CATHY (*entering*). Pigeon's.

EMILY. and that's a wild duck –

CATHY. A wild duck.

EMILY. and that . . . Who is that?

CATHY *is looking ahead at her face in an imaginary mirror.*

Oh Nelly. Who is that face in the mirror?

CATHY. Who is that face in the mirror?

EMILY/CATHY. Who is it that moved just now? And again. Who is that lady in her expensive gown?

EMILY. She asked, gazing earnestly at herself in the mirror.

PATRICK. Read on.

EMILY *(protesting)*. I do not think it –

PATRICK. Read on.

EMILY *(reading)*. And say what I could, I was incapable of making her comprehend it was her own reflection. It was herself, surrounded by feathers she had torn from her pillow.

CATHY. Who is it? I don't know her.

EMILY. I rose and covered the mirror with a shawl.

EMILY/CATHY. It is behind there still. And it stirred. Who is it? I hope it will not come out when you are gone.

CATHY. Oh Nelly, the room is haunted. I am afraid of being alone.

EMILY. It is *yourself*. Catherine Linton. Wife of Mr Edgar Linton and mistress of this fine house. You must stop this at once and come to your senses before your husband hears your nonsense.

EMILY/CATHY. She watches me. Don't leave me.

CATHY. Tell her to go away. Tell her I do not know her. Tell her I – How did she get in here?!

EMILY *(suddenly closing the manuscript)*. Father –

PATRICK. You are right. It is . . . unusual. Tonight we shall eat in the dining room and eat well. You will stay indoors and help your sister to prepare our meal. You may use the rest of the week's housekeeping. It is an occasion, is it not? I am to see my only son.

BRANWELL *as an eight-year-old, runs into the room followed by his sisters,* CHARLOTTE *and* ANNE (*aged nine and five*). *He is carrying a parcel.* PATRICK *is fully sighted as he was twenty years before. Throughout this sequence* EMILY *remains in the kitchen in July 1845, preparing supper. The children chase around the table,* BRANWELL *holding the parcel aloft.*

CHARLOTTE. What is it, Father? (*Re the parcel.*)

ANNE. Who did it come from?

BRANWELL. It says . . . It says my name.

PATRICK. Then you should open it.

BRANWELL. Me?

PATRICK. Who else?

BRANWELL. But it's not my birthday or Christmas or –

PATRICK. Ah, then I will take it back.

PATRICK *makes as if to take the parcel.* BRANWELL *snatches it back.*

BRANWELL *tears the wrapping off the parcel.*

ANNE. Let me see, let me see. What is it?

CHARLOTTE. An atlas.

ANNE. Pretty patterns. What is it for?

PATRICK. That you might know what lies beyond that hill and to where the river is flowing. These are the countries and this is the sea.

CHARLOTTE. How did they find out? How did they know?

PATRICK. They went there. They walked and rode and sailed.

ANNE. Pretty colours.

BRANWELL. So many pages. There's so much.

CHARLOTTE. Where are we?

PATRICK. Too small to be seen. There is Leeds, and London and France.

CHARLOTTE. And Belgium.

BRANWELL. Where Napoleon was defeated.

PATRICK. There are still places we know little of. These pages are yet to be detailed, but soon, soon, brave men will risk their lives to find out. Perhaps young Branwell will one day discover a continent.

ANNE *is impatient to open the second parcel.*

ANNE. Open the other one.

BRANWELL *opens the second book. The pages are blank.*

BRANWELL. Where are the words? The pictures? What shall I do with it, sir?

CHARLOTTE. Write in it.

BRANWELL. But I should not like to spoil it. You keep it.

CHARLOTTE. May I have it, Father? I should like it very much.

PATRICK. But I bought it for Branwell.

BRANWELL. What should I write?

PATRICK. Whatever is noble, whatever is righteous, whatever is – true.

BRANWELL. Tell me.

PATRICK. I shouldn't have to tell you. My father, he beat me and threw my books in the river to teach me not to waste my time. When I graduated from Cambridge he laughed at me, said I should be too clever now to come home. That they'd never see me again . . . And he was right. I never went back. I didn't mean it to be that way but the years went by and . . . and . . . there was no point in writing a letter because he couldn't read or write . . . and even if he could . . . what was there to say?

CHARLOTTE. Did you get the books back?

ANNE. Why did he throw them in the river?

PATRICK. They made him feel . . . foolish. They made him feel ashamed because he couldn't read the words. He thought that I looked down on him because I wanted something better. Because I had dreams of a different kind of life. I wanted something different for my own son.

Lights change.

BRANWELL. After one hundred days on the open seas they catch their first sight of land.

CHARLOTTE (*shouts*). A tropical island!

BRANWELL *jumps up onto the table as if standing at the prow of a ship.* CHARLOTTE *climbs up beside him.* PATRICK *returns to the kitchen, 1845. He stands over* EMILY *as she peels the potatoes.*

BRANWELL. The Commander stands at the helm and shouts for his men. (*Shouts.*) Ahoy!

CHARLOTTE. Ahoy!

BRANWELL. They see before them the mighty rocks where waves crash and splinter.

CHARLOTTE (*climbing down from the table as if entering the forest*). They are dazzled by the beauty of the island. The glittering sands stretch before the verdant rainforest. Beneath the panoply every leaf drips and sweats. There are huge pungent flowers that blaze at night and die in the morning.

BRANWELL. We can't see the rainforest until we are landed. We must announce our arrival with cannon fire and pistol shot.

CHARLOTTE. I will fire the first cannon.

BRANWELL. No. You must go down below 'til the battle is done.

CHARLOTTE. Why must I always –

BRANWELL. I told you before. The women must be kept safe and be ready to nurse us when we are wounded.

CHARLOTTE. Then I shall be a man, the Commander, and lead the great army into the bay.

BRANWELL. But *I'm* the Commander.

CHARLOTTE (*acting it out*). Until you are shot down by a mighty arrow and I must take over.

BRANWELL (*acting it out*). Until I'm brought back to life by a magic potion just as you are thrown overboard.

He throws her over his shoulder.

CHARLOTTE. Branwell, put me down! I will not play unless I may live.

BRANWELL. How can you lead the army? You don't even know what a musket is or how many men are in a battalion or –

CHARLOTTE. I don't want to know. Battles are stupid. All that ever happens is killing and being wounded over and over 'til we all die of boredom.

BRANWELL. That shows how much you know.

CHARLOTTE. Don't want to know.

BRANWELL runs off to act out the battle in a corner. We hear the muffled sounds of explosions and death cries. Then he settles and writes in his book. CHARLOTTE writes into a tiny book made of scraps tied together.

July 1845. PATRICK looks on as EMILY peels potatoes.

PATRICK. Roasted not boiled. In the fat around the meat. And a good gravy. Not too much salt. I shall need you to accompany me to afternoon and evening prayers. My curate is to go to the hospital.

EMILY looks up.

The man who lost his hand to the loom, he has become ill.

PATRICK and EMILY leave during the following.

Back in childhood, as before. BRANWELL returns to CHARLOTTE. He stands awkwardly behind her.

BRANWELL. The battle is over now and we have won and there is a feast and dancing and a beautiful daughter.

They open their writing books.

CHARLOTTE. She is tall, dark, an exquisite creature raised to enchant, to delight. The Commander watches as she dances and sings.

BERTHA *enters, dressed in a flame red dress. She sings and dances on the kitchen table, her back to the audience.*

When he speaks to her, he does so in a low voice so that she must lean close and feel his breath on her ear. He tells her that in all his life he never saw anything so beautiful.

As CHARLOTTE *continues with the description, she begins to write. She leans her notebook on* BRANWELL*'s back.* BERTHA *rolls on the kitchen table in a state of arousal.*

She feels as if her skin is splitting open like a peach that is too ripe. Her heart, like a trapped bird, batters her breast so she cannot speak.

Elsewhere, EMILY, *aged seven, and* ANNE, *aged six, are also at play. They write down the story as it comes.*

EMILY. He was awoken by the strangest of sounds. At first he thought it was the wind howling and then he heard in it a voice. 'Let me in. Let me in.'

ANNE (*frightened*). He tried at once to lock the window –

EMILY. But as he reached for the clasp, his grasp closed upon the fingers of a little ice-cold hand. He tried to draw back his arm but the hand clung to it. 'Let me in. Let me in. I'm come home. I lost my way on the moor at night. Twenty years. For twenty years I've been searching – '

ANNE, *frightened, begins to pray.*

Lights change. EMILY *then* ANNE *and* BRANWELL *kneel beside* CHARLOTTE, *also praying.* PATRICK *is distraught but trying to stay in control. His daughter Elizabeth is dead in the next room.*

PATRICK. Go to the bedroom. You are to take it in turns to say goodbye to your sister. Her eyes are closed and her breath still but she can hear you. Her spirit is in the room.

BRANWELL. What should we say, Father?

PATRICK. That you love her and will not cry for her, for she is gone to a better place. We must not try to keep her. She is not ours.

ANNE. Whose is she, Father?

PATRICK. She belongs to the Lord our God who is merciful and all loving and – wise.

EMILY. Then why must He hurt her? Why could He not take her quietly?

PATRICK. We cannot know. It is not ours to know –

EMILY. Why not?

BRANWELL. Will she see Mother?

PATRICK. She will.

CHARLOTTE. And our sister Maria?

ANNE. Cannot we go with her?

BRANWELL. Shh! Be quiet.

ANNE. What if I must cry, Father?

PATRICK. Enough. Go to her quickly and in turn. Stand in line according to age.

They stand in line with CHARLOTTE *at the front followed by* BRANWELL, *then* EMILY *and* ANNE.

Later the same day.

The four children sit together. PATRICK *can still be heard praying.*

CHARLOTTE (*reading from her writing book*). The great fleet slept in the bay like some fearsome creature tethered and bound. The cannons gathered rust and the rigging began to rot.

ANNE (*reading back what has just been written, struggling a little with the longer words*). 'Let me in. Let me in. I'm come home. I lost my way on the moor at night. Twenty years, for twenty years I've been searching.'

She looks up at EMILY *who is distracted.*

What next?

EMILY. How can we know that she is in a better place? What if she is not with Mother or Maria? What if they are all of them lost? Gone forever as if they never were, or wandering the darkness. Always alone and afraid and –

ANNE. We must not think that.

CHARLOTTE. We must trust to the Lord our God who is merciful and loving and –

EMILY. How is He merciful? How is He? It was not true that she could hear us. I looked into her eyes. She was not there –

ANNE *exits, plugging her ears.*

CHARLOTTE. Be quiet. Father will hear.

BRANWELL. When I die I will not be gone. I shall make myself famous so that they will always remember me and talk of me. I shall be a great painter or poet, just as Father intends.

CHARLOTTE (*furious*). Shut up!

BRANWELL (*brandishing sword*). Hold your tongue, fair maiden. You think you can insult the great genius Branwell? Well, think again.

BRANWELL *jumps on* CHARLOTTE *in mock battle. Suddenly she pushes him off violently.*

CHARLOTTE. You are not a genius and never will be. You're just a stupid, puny, little boy. A silly, little boy who knows nothing. Nothing.

BRANWELL. Then you are not a fair maiden and never will be. The boys at church call you the weasel but I think it too kind. The ferret, perhaps, or the rat or the –

CHARLOTTE *runs to the table and writes furiously.*

Lights change as ANNE *enters, carrying their adult clothing.*

*The women take off their children's clothes and change
back into adults as they speak. They address the audience.*

EMILY. At what moment. When is it that a girl comes to
understand her price in the marketplace?

ANNE. The tag that will for evermore hang around her neck
telling others her value.

CHARLOTTE (*writing, upset*). Weasel. Ferret. Rat.

ANNE. My sister once described herself in her diary as –

CHARLOTTE. 'Something almost repulsive.'

EMILY. At the age of twelve she told her family she would
never marry.

ANNE. But despite, or perhaps *because* of her plain face, she
wanted, from childhood, to be 'forever known'.

EMILY. She wanted to exist not as flesh and bone, not as eye
and cheek and tooth and hair but as word. To be invisible.
To steal unseen into your innermost chamber, free from her
unfortunate body. Free to be whatever she might imagine.

CHARLOTTE. Forever known. For ever known. I wrote these
words in a letter to the Poet Laureate.

*The following letter should be read aloud from a biography.
The sisters gather together to see the page.*

EMILY. My dear girl. You speak of my 'stooping from a throne
of light and glory'. You who so ardently desire to be
'forever known' as a poetess.

ANNE. The daydreams in which you indulge are likely to
produce a distempered state of mind. Literature cannot be
the business of a woman's life, and it ought not to be.

CHARLOTTE. The more she is engaged in her proper duties
the less time she will have for it even as recreation.

EMILY. To these duties you have not yet been called but when
you are, you will be less eager for celebrity.

CHARLOTTE *takes up the biography.*

CHARLOTTE. Sir, I cannot rest until I have answered your letter. At first I felt only shame that I had ventured to trouble you. A painful heat rose to my face when I thought of the quires of paper I had covered with what once gave me so much delight. The letter I wrote you was senseless trash from beginning to end. I have since endeavoured not only to observe all the duties a woman ought to fulfil but to feel deeply interested in them. (*She picks up her sewing.*) I don't always succeed for sometimes when I am sewing I'd far rather be reading or writing but I try to deny myself.

EMILY. At school Charlotte came top of her class and won a medal for good behaviour.

CHARLOTTE. Once more allow me to thank you with sincere gratitude. I trust I shall never more feel ambitious to see my name in print.

Lights change. 1833. CHARLOTTE *kneels beside her bed at Roe Head School saying her prayers. She is seventeen years old.* EMILY *enters, carrying something in her hands.*

CHARLOTTE. The bedtime bell rang an hour ago.

EMILY *sits beside the candle.*

What are you doing?

EMILY. I found it in the woods.

CHARLOTTE. You are not allowed to go to the woods. You've been told before.

EMILY. I brought it inside to see if it might live. But I think not. The wing is broken.

CHARLOTTE. It is against school rules. It is forbidden to bring animals –

EMILY. I will take it outside and kill it.

CHARLOTTE. Just leave it as it would have been left had you not – meddled –

EMILY. Then it will suffer on only to die.

CHARLOTTE. As it would have, had you not found it.

EMILY. Which I did.

CHARLOTTE (*snaps*). Do whatever you want. You always do.

EMILY *gathers up the bird and heads towards the door.*

I am told you have scarcely eaten since you arrived. Your plate returns to the kitchen as it left.

EMILY. I have not been hungry.

CHARLOTTE. And you refuse to wear your corset or petticoat.

EMILY. They are not comfortable. It does not suit me to –

CHARLOTTE. You must make it suit. You must learn to be comfortable.

EMILY. Why?

CHARLOTTE. It is necessary if you wish to be thought well of, if you wish to succeed in –

EMILY. I don't.

CHARLOTTE. Are you unhappy here? Is something the matter?

EMILY. Only that I would choose to be elsewhere.

CHARLOTTE. We cannot always choose to be as and where we would wish. We are not so rich we can live by our own rules. We must soon make our way in the world. We must learn to earn our own . . .

EMILY. I cannot bear to be told all day what to do and when to do it. To be forced to stop and start according to the bell. I have no desire to learn embroidery or copy from the board hour after hour or recite what I am told. It is boring and pointless and –

CHARLOTTE. I have here the essay you wrote for composition.

CHARLOTTE *unfolds a piece of paper from her pocket.*

(*Reads.*) In one of those moods when the world of the imagination suffers a winter which blights all its vegetation, I sat at the foot of an old oak. Amongst the branches the nightingale came to begin its song. 'Poor fool,' I said to myself. 'Is it to guide the shot to your flesh or the child to your little ones that you sing so high and so clear? Silence that inappropriate melody, huddle down in your nest or tomorrow it will be empty.'

EMILY. We were taken to the woods and told to describe what we saw. I did exactly as I was told.

CHARLOTTE (*continuing to read*). Why was man created? He tortures, he kills, he devours, he suffers, he dies –

EMILY. Give it back.

EMILY *grabs the essay and crumples it.*

CHARLOTTE. You should return home. Immediately. Anne may take your place after the vacation so that it is not wasted.

EMILY *stands holding the dying bird.*

CATHY *enters agitated, still inspecting the feathers from the torn pillow.*

CATHY. This is a . . . This is a . . . I cannot remember. A wild duck's and a pigeon's and . . .

CHARLOTTE. Go then and kill it, quickly. (*Re the dying bird.*)

EMILY. Don't think that I don't know that I have failed and despise myself for it.

EMILY *goes to the table.*

CATHY. I used once to know them all but now I am too long indoors and have forgotten.

Lights change. July 1845. EMILY, as before, sitting at the kitchen table, her writing book in front of her. She is reading back the passage she is writing, speaking the occasional word with CATHY.

CATHY talks to her maidservant NELLY. She is in a state of confusion. EMILY speaks NELLY's lines.

(*As if in front of a mirror.*) Who is that face? Who is it that moved just now? And again? Who is that lady in her expensive gown? Why are there feathers all around?

EMILY (*as* NELLY). Give over with your baby work. You know well enough who it is.

CATHY. I have seen her before but cannot remember. Tell me, Nelly.

EMILY (*as* NELLY). It is yourself. Yourself, in the mirror.

CATHY. But it cannot be.

EMILY (*as* NELLY). But it is.

CATHY. Myself!

EMILY (*as* NELLY). Who else?

CATHY. Tell her to go away. Tell her I do not know her. Tell her I . . .

EMILY (*as* NELLY). Stop that.

CATHY. Open the window again. Open it wide. Nelly, quickly. Why don't you move?

EMILY (*as* NELLY). Because I will not give you your death of cold.

CATHY. But I'm burning. I cannot breathe.

CATHY *runs to the front of the stage and pushes open the window. An icy wind fills the room.*

EMILY (*as* NELLY). Mrs Linton!

CATHY. Don't call me that. Who is that? My name is Cathy.

EMILY (*as* NELLY). You shall freeze.

CATHY (*leaning from the window and out into the winter night*). Look, that's my room back at home, with the candle burning.

EMILY (*as* NELLY). There is nothing but darkness.

CATHY. Nelly sits up late, doesn't she?

EMILY (*as* NELLY). I am here beside you.

CATHY. She's waiting 'til we come home that she may lock the gate. We have been on the moors all day and forgotten the time. She will not lock the gate until we are home. She will not lock us out, she will not.

EMILY (*as* NELLY). You are grown up and married, Mrs Linton, and live at the manor with servants and a husband who loves you and a duty to –

CATHY. Where is my husband? Why does he not come?

EMILY (*as* NELLY). He is in the library.

CATHY. The library! The library! What in the name of all that feels has he to do with books when I am dying.

EMILY (*as* NELLY). I shall go to him.

CATHY. No. No. Don't leave me. Don't leave me alone with the woman in the mirror.

EMILY (*as* NELLY). Shsh.

CATHY/EMILY (CATHY *leads with* EMILY *repeating*). I wish I were a girl again. Half-savage and hardy and free. Why am I so changed? (*In unison.*) I am sure I would be myself again were I once amongst the heather on those hills.

EMILY. Were I once amongst the heather on those hills.

Lights change. 1835. CHARLOTTE, EMILY *and* ANNE *are putting the finishing touches to a jacket they have made for* BRANWELL. *He stands on a chair wearing the jacket as they stitch the hem. He is reading from his writing book.*

BRANWELL (*as the scene is set up around him*). As the Commander set sail, the sun was rising. Every weapon shone in the early light. The cannons pointed towards the glittering horizon. He kissed goodbye to his young bride.

He turns the page.

ANNE. Be still a moment while I get it straight.

BRANWELL. Not too short. It is the fashion now to have tails and part them as you sit.

ANNE. It is made exactly according to the pattern you ordered from London.

CHARLOTTE. I read in the newspaper about a machine that will sew at twenty times our speed and every stitch perfect.

ANNE. How can it be?

CHARLOTTE. They claim it will make a skirt in an afternoon and a pillowcase in half an hour. Think of the years that would be rescued.

ANNE. But there is nothing better than the sight of a buttonhole done exactly right, or even a hem when you have taken care.

CHARLOTTE. You shall be joining Mr Ludd and destroying all machines for robbing man of his dignity.

ANNE. Perhaps I shall. They say that the noise in the mills now is so terrible it can leave a man deaf. That they must work to the speed of the machines or else risk injury. Men who had before a skilled job are sitting all day repeating one drear task a thousand times.

BRANWELL. The cloth can be made quicker and of better quality. The mills will close if they cannot compete with the market.

ANNE. And for what do we need more cloth of better quality? To dress ladies up in endless petticoats and ensure they might change three times a day.

EMILY. Have you ever thought how strange it is that we consider nakedness shameful. That we consider it quite sensible to lace women into corsets and crinolines. To torture hair with hot irons. To hide under mountains of silk and lace and whalebone. All this is considered most respectable whilst the sight of the flesh God gave us is sinful.

ANNE. There are said to be shops in London where a single bonnet costs more than a year's wages on the looms. And the style changing so often they must be discarded long before they are worn out.

BRANWELL. When people have money they wish it to be known. What better way than to dress up and make yourself an object of envy. I expect I shall see some wondrous sights in the capital.

CHARLOTTE *holds up the shirt she is working on.*

CHARLOTTE. It is strange to think that you will be there in only three days' time. That even as we sit here now, there exists that other world, those magnificent buildings, those famous streets thronging with people and life. That this very shirt will be worn in that great city.

Lights change. CHARLOTTE *continues to speak as the family rearrange themselves.* BRANWELL *stands beside an easel. He is painting the famous portrait of* CHARLOTTE, EMILY *and* ANNE *that was referred to in the Prologue.* PATRICK *sits reading a newspaper.*

You must climb to the top of Saint Paul's and sketch everything that you see. And after, walk up Fleet Street past all the great publishing houses to the Aldwych and along the Strand remembering everything that you may write and tell us exactly as it is.

ANNE. And at Saint Paul's you must put a penny in the poor box and wish that there might be no more illness in the town and that those children we saw yesterday without shoes might have some and –

CHARLOTTE. Oh! And at the National Gallery will you make a list of all the paintings and describe the style and contents of each?

BRANWELL. I shall have better things to do with my time than make lists and wishes for my sisters.

PATRICK. Spend as much time as you can in the galleries. You can learn much by looking.

BRANWELL. It shall not be long before the crowds are coming to see the great Brontë portraits.

PATRICK. The Academy expect you at nine o'clock on Monday morning. Be sure to be on time and remember your letter of commendation.

CHARLOTTE. I have put the letter and the tickets in your jacket pocket . . .

PATRICK. You will write each day to tell us that all is well.

CHARLOTTE. Not just a line. You must tell us everything you have seen since last you wrote.

PATRICK. Be sure to remember. We will be waiting on your word.

Lights change. BERTHA *appears. She waves and waves.*

CHARLOTTE. She stood upon the shore. She waved until the Commander was nothing but a speck in her eye and still she waved. That night she wept into his pillow.

A week later. EMILY *is alone in the kitchen.* BRANWELL *enters, carrying his portfolio and bags. He is wearing a new cravat. He has been drinking.*

EMILY (*startled*). You are back.

BRANWELL. Indeed.

EMILY. We had expected you yesterday, and the day before. We have had no letter since your first saying only that you had arrived.

Pause.

I will call Father.

BRANWELL. Not yet.

EMILY. You are not unwell?

BRANWELL. I am in excellent health although a little dishevelled on account of an unfortunate incident which could not be helped but has somewhat undone our best-laid plans.

Pause.

EMILY. The Academy. They did not accept you as we hoped? They did not like the pictures?

BRANWELL. They did not *see* the pictures.

EMILY. They did not see you?

BRANWELL. They did not *see* the pictures on account of the theft of my purse on the day of my arrival.

EMILY. But you wrote to say that all was well.

BRANWELL. *After* I had posted the letter.

EMILY. But why did you not –

BRANWELL. I can tell you now, London is not so great as they would have you believe. There are some fine buildings to be sure but the people are all of them in a hurry to be someplace else. Looking past like you didn't exist. Noses in the air, as if you smelt of cabbages because you are not carrying a fancy cane or an expensive hat. (*Getting heated.*) They have no right to do so, as on their own streets there are those looks as if they haven't washed for weeks. Sitting in the gutter like so much rubbish to be left to rot.

EMILY. You went to the Academy . . . but they would not see you?

BRANWELL (*barks at her*). I told you. I could not go. My purse was taken and –

EMILY. You bought yourself a new cravat.

BRANWELL. You must tell Father . . . and the others. Tell them I am gone to bed and will not be disturbed. Tell them I am much shaken and do not wish to talk of it. Do you understand? I will not be interrogated by my sisters who have themselves no idea what it takes to leave home and make their way.

EMILY *stares back at him as he turns and leaves the room.*

CHARLOTTE. That night she wept into his pillow. The next day she refused to eat. For weeks she spoke to no one, waiting only for news of his return. She locked the bedroom door and closed the shutters.

BERTHA *falls to her knees. She emits a low, hollow, mirthless laugh. She rolls on the floor, still laughing.*

Lights change.

BRANWELL. I have just received a letter of some import.

CHARLOTTE. What does it say?

BRANWELL. Some excellent news which concerns us all. I am to be part of the greatest adventure of the century. I am to witness history unfolding beneath my nose. Life as we know it will never be the same. A man will be able to wake up in London and go to sleep in Edinburgh. A letter may be delivered in Leeds on the very day it was written in York.

ANNE. Tell us. What is it?

BRANWELL. The railways are to be the lifeblood, the arteries of this country. No man need live a life of rural isolation, of ignorance and seclusion. No man need ever again long to know what lies beyond –

CHARLOTTE. We are waiting.

BRANWELL. I have here in my hand my letter of employment to commence on the first of the month when the line is to be opened by the Mayor of – Bradford.

CHARLOTTE. What is it? What is the job?

BRANWELL. Assistant to the Clerk in charge of Sowerby Bridge Railway Station on the Leeds to Manchester Railway.

Pause.

CHARLOTTE. Sowerby Bridge?

Lights change. BRANWELL *gets out his notebook and writes furiously during the following.*

EMILY. He was happy. We should have been happy for him.

CHARLOTTE. He was not.

EMILY. How do we know?

CHARLOTTE. It was at Sowerby Bridge he began to drink himself into a stupor each day. Writing endless letters to *Blackwood's Magazine* begging them to publish his poetry.

EMILY. Because he knew that we were disappointed. He knew that he had failed us. That we were ashamed.

BRANWELL (*reading*). Dear Sir. When I was a child I read your periodical and it laid a hold upon my mind which has, in succeeding years, consecrated into a sacred feeling.

CHARLOTTE. 'A sacred feeling.'

BRANWELL. My resolution is to devote my life and ability to you, and to literature. For God sake do not coldly refuse my aid. Do not turn from the truth but allow me to prove myself.

As the argument between EMILY *and* CHARLOTTE *goes on,* BRANWELL *continues to pour forth his frustration in letters to prospective publishers.*

EMILY. He had been infected by that strange sickness, the belief that life has no meaning unless it is perceived by others. Unless you sit upon a 'throne of light and glory'. 'Forever known.'

CHARLOTTE. Is it really so ridiculous to want for him a life of greater purpose, of higher thoughts, finer feelings? A view other than the office wall of Sowerby Station? The event of the day a passing train?

EMILY (*quoting* BRANWELL). 'The greatest adventure of the century.'

CHARLOTTE. He was dismissed for stealing money for drink. He drank because he went half-mad with boredom. Wandering the hills like a man lost, walking miles to the nearest tavern, desperate for company. To be 'perceived by others'. To know that he was not alone.

EMILY. Alone! Alone. We are *all* alone, and never more so than when surrounded by strangers, trying to convince them we are not the hopeless failure we believe ourselves to be.

CHARLOTTE. He was given so much.

EMILY. Too much. It was too much. We wanted too much from him.

CHARLOTTE. All of it, wasted, squandered, thrown away.

EMILY. Perhaps it is we who were lucky.

ANNE. How so?

EMILY. Perhaps it is we who should be grateful.

CHARLOTTE. For what?

EMILY. Obscurity, invisibility. That nothing was expected of us. Nothing at all. (*Beat.*) Whatever we did was our secret. Was our own.

Lights change. June 1842. CHARLOTTE *picks up a notebook of* EMILY's *poems which she has found. She looks about her to check that she is alone. She reads.*

CHARLOTTE.
Happiest when most away.
I can bear my soul from its home of clay . . .
When I am not and none beside,
Nor earth nor sea nor cloudless sky,
But only spirit wandering wide
Through infinite immensity.

EMILY *enters.*

You must forgive me. I have done something which I should not but I came upon them and began to read before I knew what they were. Once I had begun, I could not stop.

EMILY. Give them to me.

CHARLOTTE. You may be angry with me as is your right but hear me out.

EMILY. Now.

CHARLOTTE. I could not stop because they stirred in my heart such feeling . . . I know no woman ever wrote such poetry before. There is a . . . strange pathos. A music . . . wild, melancholy, utterly different from –

EMILY. Get out. Get away from me. How dare you.

CHARLOTTE. I dare because I know, I am certain that these words have uncommon power. That they must be seen, be heard. That it is a crime, a shameful waste to –

EMILY. If you ever speak of them again, either to myself or any other, I will destroy them. Do you understand?

CHARLOTTE. Hear me out. I have a proposal.

EMILY. They were written for myself and no other.

CHARLOTTE. I don't believe you.

EMILY. It is not for you to believe or not believe. It is so.

CHARLOTTE. Why write? Why sit up hour after hour into the night? I see you through the crack in the door. One, two, three o'clock. Exhausted in the morning.

EMILY. Can I not have any privacy? Can I not for one moment –

CHARLOTTE. I cannot believe, I will not believe that you don't secretly long to be read. What are words if not the means God gave us to reach, to grope towards one another through the darkness in hope, in hope of being found. In hope that we might become visible, to ourselves and others. Become known.

EMILY. Leave me alone.

CHARLOTTE. Listen to me. I have some poems of my own and Anne also. All I ask is that you allow me to send them together to a publisher and seek his opinion. We will use men's names. No one will know, but us.

EMILY. When I write, I leave behind this miserable body. I leave behind the din of the world. I forget my tedious thoughts that squabble all day like fractious children. I write to be unknown. Unknowing. To exist outside and beyond myself. To be in the . . . *is-ness* of things as I was once before I knew . . .

CHARLOTTE. What?

EMILY. . . . that the world was broken and all who live in it ashamed. Myself also.

Lights change. EMILY *goes to the table to write as* CATHY *enters with her torn pillow.* EMILY *speaks the occasional word as she writes.*

CATHY. Is that a pigeon's? Or is it a duck's? I cannot be sure. That's a turkey's and that is a . . . What is its name? They nest in the cracks on the crag. High up out of reach. Flying way above us, riding the wind, calling, making us run . . . What is it, Nelly?

CATHY/EMILY. What is it called? I must remember.

EMILY (*as* NELLY). Hush now. To bed. You must try to sleep. To rest.

CATHY. I cannot. Nelly. I am afraid I will dream. Do you ever dream?

EMILY (*as* NELLY). Now and then. I don't pay it much heed.

CATHY. I have dreamt in my life dreams that have stayed with me ever after, and changed my ideas; they've gone

CATHY/EMILY. through me and through me

CATHY. like wine into water, and altered the colour of my mind.

EMILY (*as* NELLY). Shshsh, enough.

CATHY. Last night I dreamt I had died and gone to heaven but heaven did not seem to be my home; and I broke my heart with weeping to come back to earth. The angels were so angry they threw me out into the middle of the heath where I woke, sobbing for joy.

EMILY (*as* NELLY). That's enough now.

CATHY. I had no more business to marry Edgar than I have to be in heaven. I thought I could become the wife and lady of the manor. That I could escape into another world and never more be

CATHY/EMILY. harsh or cruel or wild.

CATHY. Oh Nelly, I was wrong. I love Heathcliff, not because he is handsome, not because he is wise but because

CATHY/EMILY. he is more myself than I am.

CATHY. When he ran away, that night of the storm, the night of my engagement to Edgar, it was as if my soul was taken from me. Oh. Nelly,

CATHY/EMILY. how can I live without my life? How can I live without my soul?

ANNE *enters, folding laundry as* CHARLOTTE *goes to the front door to await the post.*

ANNE (*to* EMILY). She waits every morning for the post like some starved animal expecting the return of its master.

I have twice asked her what she is so anxious to receive and she claims it is a book she has ordered from Leeds. When I asked her what it was, she became very vague and could not remember so much as its title.

EMILY (*coming to her*). Shshshsh.

ANNE. Last week, I saw her go three times to the post office only to return with the letter still in her hand and burn it.

EMILY. In her last term, she became much taken with our tutor. He gave her some advice and a little praise which it seems she cannot now live without.

Lights change. CHARLOTTE *sits at her desk.* MR HEGER *addresses the class. He is holding* CHARLOTTE's *homework in his hand.*

HEGER. There is too much embellishment, Miss Brontë. The adjectives are so many that one confuses the other, like a garden where too much is planted and nothing may grow.

CHARLOTTE. I had thought to make it . . . interesting, sir.

HEGER. Interesting! What use have I with interesting? Words are not to be squandered, strewn about like so much confetti. So much decoration. They are the very muscle, the sinew of the language.

CHARLOTTE. You told us to –

HEGER. You must all choose your words as you would choose a weapon, that it may do precisely as you intend. Economy. Restraint. Sacrifice everything that does not contribute to clarity. Only when you have control, purpose, precision. Only then can you let the reins fly. Describe to me, Miss Brontë, the evening sky that you see from the window.

CHARLOTTE (*flatly*). It's cloudy and . . . looks as if it might rain.

HEGER. Be more specific. Describe to me this particular sky which is unlike any other sky because it is seen by you as you never have been before and never will be again.

CHARLOTTE. The clouds are . . . heavy with foreboding –

HEGER. No, no, no. It must take us by surprise. If it is familiar, we feel nothing. See nothing.

He indicates for CHARLOTTE *to continue.*

CHARLOTTE. There are clouds threatening overhead –

HEGER. Every word must be chosen, not only for its meaning but for its particular charge, its unique atmosphere and subtle associations, the sound it makes when spoken, the feel of it in the mouth –

CHARLOTTE (*defiant*). Angry clouds threaten overhead, their edges shot through, livid with the flame of the evening.

HEGER (*indicates she should stand*). More.

CHARLOTTE. I never before saw such a fiery light, as if the clouds were embers just blown by a mighty wind. I felt at once such a swelling in my throat, such impatience of restraint. Such a strong wish for wings, an urgent thirst to see, to know, to feel –

HEGER. You see? The words surprise us and yet it is as if we have always known them to be true. We recognise the truth as if all experience were shared and we were part of some great being that is all mankind.

The bell rings for the end of the lesson. CHARLOTTE *gets up to go.* MR HEGER *calls her back and indicates for her to sit. She does so.*

Here you are in your classroom. You sit and look at your tutor as you are bid. You wait obediently to be dismissed. And yet, what do I know of your thoughts? What does any being know of what takes place in the head of another?

When God made man, He gave us not only the power to see but the knowledge that we could *be* seen, and with it came the desire to hide, to show only what is admirable, what is enviable in ourselves. To conceal that of which we are ashamed. But read a good book and you are allowed to enter. To see as if through the eyes of another. To know their thoughts. Their deepest, their darkest fears and longings.

The bell rings again. He leaves as she watches him.

Lights change. Some weeks later. CHARLOTTE *is alone at home. She writes to* MR HEGER. BERTHA *enters, no longer young and beautiful, but ravaged by years of madness and incarceration. She crawls towards* CHARLOTTE.

CHARLOTTE. Dear Sir. Day and night I find neither rest nor peace. For three months I have waited and still you torture me with no reply. Nothing. Not a morsel. Not a mouthful. It is cruel. The poor need little to live. They ask only for the crumbs that fall from the table. Deny them this and they die of hunger.

She screws up the letter and starts again.

Dear Sir. In your last letter you told me of the snowdrops you could see from your window.

She crosses it out furiously. BERTHA *is behind* CHARLOTTE, *wild with longing and frustration.*

I love you. I love you. I love you. You can't do this to me. If I was a dog you wouldn't do this to me. I wish I was your dog so I could follow you and smell you and eat the scraps that you throw under the table and lick your shoes and have you beat me and –

She realises what she has said and stops herself, horrified.

Oh God.

She screws up the letter, throwing it to the floor. BERTHA *flings herself to the ground.*

Oh Lord, forgive me.

CHARLOTTE *picks up a mirror.*

A greater fool than I never breathed the breath of life. Me, a favourite with him? Me, gifted with the power of pleasing him? Me, of importance to him in any way? Look at that tired, uneven, charmless face and draw it with chalk onto a piece of paper. Afterwards mix your finest tints and paint the loveliest face you can imagine. Whenever in future you imagine he once thought well of you, take out these two pictures and compare them.

Lights change. ANNE *and* CHARLOTTE *go to pick up the post.* CHARLOTTE *gets there first.* CHARLOTTE *picks up a letter and reads the envelope. She is disappointed. She gives* ANNE *the letter and goes to leave.* EMILY *is in the hallway.*

ANNE. It did not come?

Beat.

The book?

CHARLOTTE. No.

ANNE. Are you alright?

CHARLOTTE. Can I not pick up the post without the two of you whispering and insinuating behind my back? Can I not do anything in this house without being stared at as if I were some kind of freak, some kind of lunatic.

ANNE. We didn't mean to –

CHARLOTTE (*shouts*). Leave me alone.

CHARLOTTE runs from the room. They continue to fold the laundry.

ANNE (*to* EMILY). Perhaps it is as well that she is to go away.

EMILY. Perhaps.

ANNE. Spring is coming. Let us hope her pupils are curious and have a will to learn. They may provide her cure.

Lights change. Two months later. CHARLOTTE *arrives home in coat and shawl with luggage. She sneezes.* ANNE *gives her a hanky as she continues her story.*

CHARLOTTE. They talk of nothing but the day they will marry and wish only to learn what will win them a wealthy husband. They are both pretty as little kittens. They pity me, I am certain. How, they wonder, would life be bearable with a plain face and a dreary dress. One night they took it upon themselves to dress me up and would not be persuaded against it. The ordeal took an entire evening. It was clear, however, that in spite of their enthusiasm, nothing suited. I was not improved one bit. When I said as much, they became sulky and rude and blamed me for looking miserable. The next day I was given notice.

ANNE. I'm sorry.

EMILY. It is them we should pity. To be beautiful is to be cursed. To belong not to yourself but others.

CHARLOTTE (*turning out her purse*). I have earned five pounds and ten pence. Almost exactly the price of the gig there and back.

ANNE. It was not your fault.

CHARLOTTE. I will advertise again tomorrow.

ANNE. But you're unwell. You must wait until you are . . . better.

CHARLOTTE. There are bills to be paid.

ANNE. We are leaving tomorrow, Branwell and I.

CHARLOTTE. Tomorrow!

ANNE. We will earn enough in three months to pay what is owed and some more beside.

CHARLOTTE. Where is he?

ANNE. Upstairs, packing his trunk.

CHARLOTTE. He is to be trusted?

EMILY. He wishes to make amends.

ANNE. What better way than to pay his own debts through honest toil. To devote himself to a growing boy who must be taught by example.

CHARLOTTE. You are leaving in the morning?

ANNE. At eight o'clock.

CHARLOTTE. So soon?

ANNE (*brimming with anticipation*). It is strange to think that this time tomorrow, everything that I look upon will be different. The faces, the trees, the ground beneath my feet. A whole world that I cannot now imagine and yet I will so soon be there and no longer here.

EMILY. Poor love.

ANNE. No. No. I am happy to go. I feel as if my whole life I have been waiting for this moment. To be of use to someone. I am sick of being useless. Thinking only of my own selfish hopes and fears. From tomorrow I will think only of what will benefit my charges. Of their care and improvement. They are young and not yet spoiled by thoughts of marriage. I may do much to encourage and a little to inspire. Forgive me, I am excited and full of foolish thoughts. No doubt I shall be much sobered in the morning when the time comes to go. But tomorrow, do not take my tears for sadness. I am only too full of hope and gratitude.

Lights change. July 1845. The sound of pouring rain. Late evening on the night of BRANWELL *and* ANNE*'s return from Thorpe Green. They have been delayed by a storm.* EMILY *is alone in the kitchen, reading by candlelight. As* CHARLOTTE *enters there is a huge crack of thunder.*

CHARLOTTE. I told Father he should sleep. He worries that they are so long delayed.

EMILY. Go to bed, I will wait up.

CHARLOTTE. Emily. Let me see Anne's letter, I would rather know the worst.

EMILY. I told you.

CHARLOTTE. Please.

EMILY. She asked me to keep it to myself.

CHARLOTTE. What does it matter, I shall know soon enough.

EMILY. Then let it be.

CHARLOTTE, *exasperated, begins to clear the table.*

ANNE (*entering, calling from the front door*). I'm home.

EMILY *and* CHARLOTTE *run to the door. They remove* ANNE*'s sodden coat as they speak.*

CHARLOTTE. You're soaking.

ANNE. The coach was delayed by the storm. The roads are like rivers and the rivers like seas. I never saw such rain.

CHARLOTTE. And Branwell?

ANNE. He is bringing our trunks with the coachman. He has to pay for the gig.

CHARLOTTE. Take off your clothes. Come to the fire.

ANNE. I am here at last. I cannot tell you how often I have imagined this room, and here I am. Here you are.

CHARLOTTE. You are thinner.

ANNE. How is Father?

EMILY. Asleep. He will see you tomorrow.

CHARLOTTE. You must be hungry. We cooked a roast and a plum pudding.

ANNE. I couldn't eat. I am too exhausted. I would rather carry stones up a mountain, scrub floors 'til my hands are raw, anything, than spend another day in that exquisite nursery with those . . . impossible . . . Yesterday I found the boy trying to drown a kitten in a bucket of water. When I asked him why, he said he had never seen anything die and wished to do so.

CHARLOTTE. And Branwell? He is dismissed?

ANNE. The master has threatened to shoot him should he ever set eyes upon his wife again.

EMILY. How was it found out?

ANNE. She had tried to put an end to it. Last Friday, Branwell left a note to her on her dressing table and her husband found it.

BRANWELL (*appearing, speaking the letter aloud*). Do you think I can bear to go on without you? Do you think I want to live with every day a wasteland? Every thought a torment? Every hour an eternity? Do not leave me in this abyss. I cannot live without my life. I cannot live without my soul.

CHARLOTTE. How long has this been going on?

ANNE. A year. Maybe more. He came to me one night saying that he could keep it a secret no longer.

BRANWELL *speaks to* ANNE *in a state of joyous excitement. The sisters continue in the kitchen as if imagining* BRANWELL's *words.* BERTHA *crawls towards* CHARLOTTE.

BRANWELL. I never knew a woman capable of such sweet fever, such secret hunger. She likes for me to force her against her will. And all the time protesting and struggling and talking of her husband and her honour.

CHARLOTTE. In her own house. Her children's tutor.

BERTHA *rolls on the ground, aroused, near* CHARLOTTE.

BRANWELL. She will sob and cry for me to stop all the while trembling with excitement. Afterwards she weeps like a child, poor love. Tells me that she never loved 'til now. That her marriage was a sham and forced upon her. That she has suffered such loneliness, such grief, such longing.

CHARLOTTE. It is shameful. Unforgiveable.

BRANWELL. She calls me her saviour.

CHARLOTTE. Beneath the same roof.

BRANWELL. Her angel.

CHARLOTTE. Like animals.

BRANWELL. Her only love. (*He exits.*)

CHARLOTTE. Has he not an ounce of self-control? Not a thought for anything but his own insatiable appetite?

EMILY. How is he now?

ANNE. One minute desperate, claiming his life to be over and not worth living without her. The next, he runs on wildly. He thinks that soon her husband will die and she will be free to marry him. He tells me he has begun to write it all down. That he is inspired as never before. That it will make a great novel.

Beat.

What of our own efforts? There is no news?

EMILY. The poems were returned again this morning with much useful advice.

CHARLOTTE. Don't ask.

EMILY (*changing the subject*). At Easter, you saw the sea.

ANNE. And what a strange and awesome thing it is. Don't ask me to describe it. I have tried and failed a hundred times. Nor is it ever the same twice. You can watch it for hours. Lose yourself in it. We must go together. All of us. When Father has had his operation and Branwell is well again.

CHARLOTTE (*looking towards the front door*). Where is he? You said he would come directly.

EMILY. Has he money?

ANNE. Yes. She gave it to him. Far more than he was owed. He paid the coachman twice the fare and tipped the porter more than a week's wages.

CHARLOTTE *goes to get her coat.*

CHARLOTTE. I'll go.

ANNE. No.

CHARLOTTE. Why not?

EMILY. Stay. He may yet come. Wait a while.

CHARLOTTE. Until it's too late.

ANNE. He will not thank you. He is little disposed to reason right now. It may be better to leave him to himself.

CHARLOTTE. To drink himself into a stupor. To tell half the town of his conquest. To spend every penny in his purse.

EMILY. If he so wishes.

CHARLOTTE. What?

EMILY. If he so wishes.

CHARLOTTE (*furious*). Why? Why do you have to oppose me at every turn? Why must you always take some absurd contradictory position just to . . . just to . . . Why can you not, for once, for once in your life behave like a reasonable, like a normal –

EMILY. He is not a child.

CHARLOTTE. Meaning?

EMILY. He will do and say as he wishes. It is not for us to police him.

CHARLOTTE. We should stand by and watch him shame his family? Watch him destroy himself?

EMILY. Perhaps he has good reason to do so.

CHARLOTTE. Indeed.

EMILY. Perhaps if you or I had suffered such a blow, we too might wish it.

CHARLOTTE. I'm going.

EMILY. Perhaps if we had lost everything in this world that made life bearable, we too might wish to forget, to pretend, to drink ourselves to oblivion. To do whatever it takes . . . We cannot say. We do not know. We can only try to imagine.

CHARLOTTE *stares at* EMILY *and then leaves into the storm.*

End of Act One.

ACT TWO

As before the interval. EMILY and ANNE are alone in the kitchen. CHARLOTTE has just left. ANNE weeps. EMILY comes to her.

ANNE. I have been so long away. I am not myself.

EMILY. Shshshsh. You are home.

ANNE. There have been things I dared not look upon for the ache . . . Stars at night. Rivers. Even the dogs I would not pet for fear of weeping. The springtime made me sick with longing. As if I had swallowed a stone and it had stuck in my throat.

EMILY. You're here. You're home.

ANNE. Your letters I would sometimes save for days. Wanting and not wanting that sweet torture. To hear the voice of one who knows you when you are surrounded by strangers. By those with whom you have no sympathy. To whom you are an oddity. A curiosity. I cannot blame them for I have become as strange to myself as I am no doubt to them. I have discovered how much of me lies not in myself but in others. In those few who know me. Without them I am a strange, brittle, humourless creature best avoided.

EMILY. I don't believe it.

ANNE. No. No. Don't make me cry. How are *you*? Tell me about you. Everything. Let me forget about myself. I am sick of myself. Tell me.

EMILY. I have taught the hawk to return.

ANNE. You have!

EMILY. Last week. For the first time. It was terrifying, to let him go. I thought he had gone. I kept calling and calling and then, just as I had given up hope . . .

ANNE. Tomorrow. I will see for myself.

EMILY. Sometimes . . . when he flies . . . It's hard to describe. It's as if I were . . . with him. As if I were no longer contained here but in . . . everything. (*Beat.*) I'm writing.

CATHY *pulls feathers from the pillow.*

Every morning I wake afraid that it will leave me. I know not where it comes from but still it comes. More like a dream than a story.

ANNE. You will read it to me. We will start tomorrow evening.

EMILY. And you? You said in your letter you had finished the first chapter.

ANNE. I cannot promise it has any merit beyond that it saved my sanity. But even that is not yet certain. You will have to let me know in a day or two.

EMILY. What is it about?

ANNE. A woman who is married and bound for life to a drunken adulterer. I intend it as provocation to those who would have women treated as children. The more I see, the more I am certain we ruin both girls and boys by insisting on the frailty of our sex. While young men must endlessly prove themselves, *we* are kept like overgrown infants in the nursery of life, our talents wasted, our energy squandered on meaningless tasks, peering out at a world we will never know –

There is a knock at the back door which opens straight into the kitchen. ARTHUR BELL NICHOLLS (PATRICK BRONTË's *curate*) *puts his head around the door. He is wet, having walked several miles in the rain. He removes his hat.*

BELL NICHOLLS. Forgive me for intruding.

EMILY. Mr Bell Nicholls.

EMILY *busies herself. She wants him to go.*

BELL NICHOLLS. Miss Emily. I wished only to welcome Miss Anne and let it be known that I am on hand should your father need me in the morning before service.

EMILY. Of course.

ANNE. Thank you.

BELL NICHOLLS. I have just returned from the hospital.
(*Pause, in which he hopes to be asked to say more.*) It was,
as we feared, too little, too late.

EMILY (*to* ANNE). A weaver lost his hand to the loom.

BELL NICHOLLS. At least he is at peace. It's his family who
will suffer. A baby born only a week ago and five others to
feed. Tomorrow we shall pray for them.

ANNE. I'm sorry.

BELL NICHOLLS. I fear it will cause further unrest in the
town. There are men gathered at the factory gates.

He waits awkwardly as if hoping to be asked into the room.
EMILY *tidies furiously, avoiding all eye contact.*

I shall see you all at church in the morning.

ANNE. Of course.

He bows and leaves, closing the door behind him.

EMILY. The new curate, Mr Arthur Bell Nicholls. He arrived
last month and has taken to calling several times a day. He
will soon no doubt tire of his enthusiasm and let us be.

ANNE. We must go tomorrow to see the weaver's widow. What
right have I to be weeping for myself when a man has died
and a family left destitute? If we thought less of ourselves
and more of others how much happier might we be.

EMILY. That their pain is greater does not make yours less.

ANNE. It should. Right now, in our own town, there are those
who have not enough to eat.

EMILY. You have read the papers?

ANNE. Is it as bad as they say?

EMILY. I have not been that way for weeks. I cannot bear to
be asked for money and have nothing to give. There are
men who have worked all their lives, sitting at the roadside.

CHARLOTTE *enters through the front door. She comes into the kitchen and removes her wet shawl in silence.*

CHARLOTTE. He made at first as if he had not seen me and continued in the telling of his tale. He had of course a captive audience, having bought them all a drink and promised more. He made a great show of introducing me to the entire party, as if I didn't know every one of them like the back of my hand, and invites me to join them, adding that I might learn a thing or two. There was a great roar of laughter as I made my way. (*She lights a candle to take upstairs.*) We will have to wait up. He mustn't wake Father. I will not have him wake Father.

Later the same night. EMILY *staggers into the hallway carrying* BRANWELL *on her back. He slips from her shoulders to the ground. He is very drunk and still drinking.* CHARLOTTE *and* ANNE *try to help him to his feet. He shakes them off and swaggers into the kitchen. From the beginning of the scene* CHARLOTTE *and* BRANWELL *are pitted against one another.*

BRANWELL. To what do I owe this great and unexpected pleasure? My three dear sisters awake at two o'clock in the morning to welcome me back into the bosom of –

ANNE. We need cold water. Fetch a towel. I'll get the bucket.

ANNE *and* EMILY *go to get a towel and bucket of water.*

BRANWELL. Cold water! A bucket! Is that any way to greet your beloved brother who you have not seen this last –

CHARLOTTE. You're drunk and reeking.

BRANWELL. I have indeed had a drink, or two, with my friends who are in fine high spirits on account of my unexpected return. They at least have missed me and are pleased to –

CHARLOTTE. We have been waiting for you. A meal was prepared. Father was expecting –

BRANWELL. I have no appetite.

CHARLOTTE. I should think not.

BRANWELL. I cannot eat because I am sick with grief.

CHARLOTTE. Because you have been dismissed from your post and are in disgrace.

BRANWELL. Disgrace! Disgrace. Listen how she says the word. Like filth in the mouth that must be spat out for fear of contamination.

CHARLOTTE. We must go to bed. You can explain yourself in the morning.

BRANWELL. Explain myself. Oh, I shall look forward to that. Because, dear Charlotte, everything must be 'explained' must it not?

ANNE has returned with a bucket of water.

ANNE. Help me sit him down.

BRANWELL. I am loved by a beautiful, an exceptional woman. A woman of great distinction. Of the highest sensibility –

CHARLOTTE. Who has defiled herself in her own home, under the nose of her children, her husband. Who has sinned against God and all that is –

BRANWELL suddenly grabs CHARLOTTE's skirt, pulling her up against him. BERTHA enters.

BRANWELL. Defiled. Oh yes, and wouldn't you like to know what that felt like? Wouldn't you?

He holds her fast, pushing his hand down between her legs.

CHARLOTTE. Leave me alone.

ANNE. Let her go.

BRANWELL (*continuing his assault*). You think I don't know. You think I can't smell it. That hot little itch, under the bedclothes. Always burning, like a rash, a scab that won't heal. Wet, weeping, raw from the scratching. The fingers in the night. Can't leave off. Itching. Twitching. What you wouldn't do to be defiled. How sweet it sounds –

EMILY and ANNE try to pull him away. He throws CHARLOTTE to the floor.

ANNE. Stop it. Stop it.

CHARLOTTE *on her knees.* BERTHA, *also on all fours.*

BERTHA. Me love you. Me love you. Me love you. You can't
do this to me. If I was a dog you wouldn't do this to me. I
wish I was your dog so I could follow you and smell you
and eat the scraps that you throw under your table and lick
your shoes and have you beat me.

CHARLOTTE. You're disgusting.

BRANWELL. You're rotten. Rotting inside. Rank. Reeking.
Stinking of – loneliness.

ANNE. That's enough.

CHARLOTTE. How dare you? How dare you humiliate me
because I have had no life. Have had to live half-starved. Had
to sacrifice everything so that you could . . . You could . . .

BRANWELL. Yes?

ANNE. You'll wake Father.

CHARLOTTE. You had everything. Had it all. Had only to
reach out and take and it would be yours. But no. We must
watch you, again and again, mess it up, waste it, throw it all
away. All we wanted was for you to succeed. To be a
success. You were our shining star. Our greatest hope. We
wanted you to burn, to burn in the darkness. For a little
light, a little light to fall on us.

BRANWELL. I don't believe you.

CHARLOTTE. It's true.

BRANWELL. You're a liar.

ANNE. Branwell.

BRANWELL. You never.

ANNE. Please . . .

BRANWELL. You wanted me to fail.

CHARLOTTE. How could you know? How could you possibly
know? You who have feasted on life. Satisfied every whim,

every desire. Who have only to ask to be given. How could you know what it is to give everything? To look on from the shadows? To watch and wait and hope against hope as he squanders every chance, ruins every opportunity?

BRANWELL. I know because every morsel that I ate was taken from your plate. Every bite, stolen. Taken from under your nose. Snatched away. I was a thief, a fraudster, a liar, a cheat. Stealing my life from you. What impossible heights I would have to reach to justify my crime. And with you. All of you watching. Always disappointed. Never enough. How could it be enough? If it hurt to watch my failure, how much worse would it have been to see me succeed? To see me take what you wanted, what you craved for yourself? What you –

CHARLOTTE. Always everyone else's fault. Never your own. Never.

He grabs her again in an embrace, half-loving, half-crushing.

BRANWELL. What do you know? What do you know about life? About the passion and the ecstasy. About the mess and the fear. Nothing. Defiled. We are all defiled. We are born drenched in blood and bile. Born guilty. Born ashamed.

CHARLOTTE *prays.*

There is no God. He is not there. He cannot hear you. There is only us. Us and the darkness.

PATRICK*'s voice is heard as he feels his way down the stairs in his dressing gown.*

PATRICK. What is the meaning of this?

BRANWELL *tries to smooth his hair and tuck in his shirt.*

BRANWELL. It is I, Father. I am home.

PATRICK. What is this noise?

BRANWELL. We had a wretched journey and are only just now arrived. Don't let us disturb you. We shall see you in the morning.

PATRICK. Where is my son?

BRANWELL. I am here, Father. I am come back.

PATRICK. Where is my son? Where is the boy I once adored? Who is this stranger in my house? Who is this shouting and swearing and stinking of –

BRANWELL. Forgive me, Father, for causing you –

PATRICK. To bed. All of you. Not another sound. Not another murmur. Do you understand?

CHARLOTTE/BRANWELL/ANNE/EMILY. Yes, Father.

The Brontë children mutter consent as they disappear towards their bedrooms.

Lights change. BERTHA, *left alone on stage, walks forward and then lies down.* CHARLOTTE *enters with a sheet. She lies on the ground using* BERTHA *as her pillow.*

BRANWELL *enters.*

BRANWELL. Forgive me, Talli. Forgive. I am all sorryness and repentance. Tell me of something that will make me happy.

CHARLOTTE. Go to bed.

BRANWELL. Tell me a story. Make me forget. Tell me another story so that my own might be forgotten a while. Make me forget about myself.

CHARLOTTE (*sitting up*). Shshshsh.

BRANWELL. Tell me about the islanders. What has become of them? What has become of our beautiful island, what of our great fleet, our brave Commander? What happened to him?

CHARLOTTE. He married the beautiful daughter. Bertha.

BRANWELL. Were they happy?

CHARLOTTE. For a while.

BRANWELL. And then? (BRANWELL *puts his head on her lap.*)

CHARLOTTE. Not so happy.

BRANWELL. Why not?

CHARLOTTE. She was mad.

BRANWELL. How mad?

CHARLOTTE. As a snake.

BRANWELL. Shame.

CHARLOTTE. Yes.

BRANWELL. What did he do?

CHARLOTTE. He brought her back to England and locked her up in a room at the top of the house and tried to forget about her.

BERTHA (*emerging from behind* CHARLOTTE, *crawling across the stage*). Can't do this to me. If I were a dog you wouldn't do this to me. Wish I was your dog. Follow you. Smell you. Sleep at the bottom of your bed. Eat the scraps you throw under your table. Lick your shoes and have you beat me . . .

CHARLOTTE *sees* BERTHA *for the first time. She stares at the creature, both fascinated and repelled.* BRANWELL *is asleep.*

Beat me. Hurt me. Make me. Sorry. I'm so sorry.

BRANWELL (*sleeping*). Sorry, I'm sorry, I . . .

BERTHA. So bad. So hurting. So much want. So much. Can't . . .

CHARLOTTE. What it was, whether beast or human being, one could not tell.

CHARLOTTE *continues to speak over* BERTHA, *who whispers.*

BERTHA. Want you. Want you I. Want. Hot little itch. Wound weeping. Red, raw from the scratching. Won't stop. Can't stop. Help me. Want me. Want me. Make me. Sorry. I'm sorry I.

CHARLOTTE. It grovelled on all fours. It snatched and growled like some strange wild animal . . . A quantity of dark grizzled hair, wild as a mane, hid its head and face.

BERTHA. No God. No love. No more. Nothing. Lost. Lost it. Can't find. Once was once.

ROCHESTER *enters.* BERTHA *retreats to a corner.*

ROCHESTER. Stand back, she sees me. Stay out of the way . . .

ROCHESTER *advances toward* BERTHA. *He stretches out his hand.* BERTHA *whimpers, her eyes filling with tears. She reaches out toward him, nuzzling his hand. She tries suddenly to kiss him on the mouth but* ROCHESTER *pushes her away, appalled.* BERTHA *clings to him, becoming increasingly sexual.* ROCHESTER *struggles to free himself. She bites him violently. He throws her down.* CHARLOTTE *stands beside* ROCHESTER *as* JANE.

That is my wife, whom I married fifteen years ago in Spanish Town, Jamaica. And this – (*Indicating* CHARLOTTE *as* JANE.) this is what I wished to have. Jane Eyre, this young girl who stands so quiet, so grave at the gate of hell. Look at the difference. Compare this sweet form, these dear eyes, this angel with that animal. Then judge me.

Lights change. Ticking clock. PATRICK *wraps himself in a blanket and sits with his back to the audience.* CHARLOTTE *sits at the table, writing.* EMILY *and* ANNE *enter.*

EMILY. For five weeks after the removal of his cataracts, Father lay in the darkness. The surgeon forbade him to move from his bed. She positioned her page so that a shaft of light from the crack between the curtains fell across it.

ANNE. Did he hear the sound of her pen as it scratched across the paper? Did he ever ask her what she was doing?

CHARLOTTE *is writing the scene as it is played. She speaks* JANE's *lines.*

PATRICK *stands and turns. He is now* ROCHESTER.

CHARLOTTE (*agitated*). You see now how the case stands, do you not? After that unholy, degrading marriage, that hideous charade. After half a lifetime of misery and solitude, I found what I can truly love.

ROCHESTER. I found you. My sympathy, my better self, my good angel, my –

CHARLOTTE (*as JANE*). Don't speak any more of those days, sir. I must not listen.

ROCHESTER. Do you mean to go one way in this world and let me go another?

CHARLOTTE (*as JANE*). I do.

ROCHESTER. Jane. (*Holding her face in his hands.*) Do you mean it now?

CHARLOTTE (*as JANE*). I do.

ROCHESTER (*kissing her neck*). And now?

CHARLOTTE (*as JANE, trying but failing to remove herself*). I do.

ROCHESTER (*wild with frustration*). Never, never was anything at once so frail and so indomitable. A reed she feels in my hand. I could bend her with my fingers, crush her with my fist, but what good would it do? Whatever I do to the cage, I cannot get at the creature. You, you exquisite, you unearthly thing. My saviour. My angel. My –

CHARLOTTE (*as JANE, violently tearing herself away*). You must not say those words to me. I must not listen to them. I have been vain, deluded, drunk with desire. The more unloved, the more solitary, the more friendless I am, the better. I will atone. I will hold to my Maker, my God, our Father. I must cling to the truth that I knew when I was sane, not mad as I am now.

Lights change as ROCHESTER *sits, turning back into* PATRICK. *The clock ticks.* PATRICK *speaks in the real world.*

PATRICK. It is warm. Open the window a little. And fetch a glass of cold water. When you return you may continue with Isaiah, just where we left off.

CHARLOTTE. Yes, Father.

Lights change as ANNE *and* EMILY *gather around* CHARLOTTE. *She is reading* Jane Eyre *aloud to them at the kitchen table. They read by candlelight.*

Not a human being that ever lived was loved better than I. And the man who loved me, I worshipped. And yet I must renounce that love. I must hold to the law given by God. It is not for times when there is no temptation. It is for that hour when the veins run fire, when the body rises in mutiny, the heart batters its cage. Oh Lord, forgive me. I will atone.

Lights change. The sisters shift positions at the table. EMILY *reads from* Wuthering Heights.

CATHY *appears. She is close to death, delirious. She runs into* HEATHCLIFF's *arms. They cling to one another.*

EMILY. Heathcliff neither spoke nor loosed his hold for some five minutes. I saw that he could hardly bear to look into her face. He knew the instant he beheld her, she was fated, sure to die.

CATHY/EMILY. I wish I could hold you 'til we both were dead. I shouldn't care what you suffered. Why shouldn't you suffer? *I* do.

HEATHCLIFF. Be silent.

CATHY. You have killed me, killed me and thriven on it. See, see how strong you are. Well, I shall soon be gone and you will forget me and live a long and happy life.

HEATHCLIFF. Don't torture me 'til I am mad as yourself. Do you think I can bear to go on without you? Do you think I want to live with every day a wasteland. Every thought a torment. Every hour an eternity.

EMILY (*as* NELLY). You must go now. The master approaches.

CATHY. No. Don't go. Don't go.

EMILY (*as* NELLY). You must. I can see him now at the gate.

HEATHCLIFF (*still clutching* CATHY *to him*). Let him come. I will crush his skull as I would a sparrow's egg. I will split his skin upon my knuckles. I will –

CATHY. The thing that irks me most is this shattered prison. I am tired of being enclosed here. I am weary to escape into that other, that higher world, and to be always there, not seeing it dimly through tears but really with it and in it. Soon I shall be beyond, beyond and above – above you all . . .

HEATHCLIFF. Catherine Earnshaw, may you not rest as long as I am living. You say I killed you. Haunt me then. Be with me always. Take any form, drive me mad, only do not leave me in this abyss where I cannot find you. Oh God. I cannot live without my life. I cannot live without my soul.

Lights change. ANNE *writes.*

ANNE. It was not until long after midnight that we heard Arthur's carriage on the driveway, at last he came, slowly and stumblingly, making noise enough for all the servants to hear. It is not enough to say I no longer love my husband. I hate him.

ARTHUR HUNTINGTON *staggers into the room. He is drunk. He leans on the back of* ANNE*'s chair as she writes.* ANNE *reads as* ARTHUR *speaks.*

ARTHUR/ANNE. To whom do I owe this great and unexpected pleasure? My own dear wife still awake at two o'clock in the morning to welcome me back into the bosom of my –

He tries to kiss ANNE (*as his wife*). *She pushes him away.*

ANNE (*as his wife, to the maid*). Run his head under cold water. Fetch a towel and a bucket.

ARTHUR. Cold water! A bucket! Is that any way to greet your beloved husband who you have not seen this last month. Tell me, have you missed me?

He pushes his hand up under her skirt. He tries to pull her towards him. She resists. He unbalances and falls.

ANNE (*as his wife*). You are drunk and reeking.

He exits as there is a knock at the back door. ARTHUR BELL NICHOLLS *appears in the doorway.*

BELL NICHOLLS. Forgive this late intrusion. Your brother is . . . there has been further unrest at the factory. A cloth cart

set alight by a picket as it was leaving the mill. He got into
a fight. It seems he has had some kind of a fit and –

EMILY. Where is he? I'll go.

BELL NICHOLLS. He is confused and talking strangely. He
thought the burning cart the devil's chariot.

EMILY. I will come with you.

The front door crashes open. BRANWELL *enters,
staggering. He is cut and bleeding. He speaks as if
confiding secret information.*

BRANWELL. Blow out the candle. Drench the fire. They are
coming. All of them. Close behind. You must lock the doors
and windows. When they come, make no sound. Don't
answer the door. Whatever they say, don't answer the door.
They have come to kill me.

CHARLOTTE. That's enough.

BRANWELL. Shshshsh.

EMILY (*holding* BRANWELL *by the shoulders*). You are
home and safe and no one can harm you.

ANNE. Sit him down. We should wash his wound and see how
deep it runs.

CHARLOTTE. Thank you, Mr Nicholls. You may go.

BRANWELL (*accosting* BELL NICHOLLS *as he tries to
leave*). Mr Nicholls. Go to the chemist. Tell them that I
need a small amount of laudanum or else I cannot, I will not
survive the night.

CHARLOTTE. Mr Nicholls, you are no longer needed.

BRANWELL. Tell them, tell them I will pay for it in the
morning.

BELL NICHOLLS. God bless you and help you. I'll see what
I can do.

BRANWELL (*whispering to* BELL NICHOLLS). Don't go.
They are trying to poison me. My sisters, they did it before
but I would not eat what they gave me. They wish to be rid

of me. I cannot blame them. I am a useless creature. All the good I saw once in myself and the world, it is gone. I would be quite happy to leave this life. To go elsewhere, were it not to the devil. (*Suddenly frantic, as if the devil were about to enter the house.*) He is following me. I saw him just now in the town.

CHARLOTTE. Thank you. Thank you, Mr Nicholls. Good night.

He exits.

BRANWELL *slumps back into a chair as the sisters try to restrain him.* ANNE *begins to wash the wound on* BRANWELL's *head.* EMILY *loosens his collar.* BERTHA *appears on the stairs. As* BRANWELL *speaks,* BERTHA *writhes and* CHARLOTTE *tears cloth for bandages.*

BRANWELL. I used once to be loved by a beautiful woman. But she had a husband and he had a gun. (*Reaching for* ANNE *as if she were his mistress.*) Tell her, tell her I think of her night and day. Her flesh, her smell, the deep, dark places where I drank. Where I drowned in her –

BERTHA. Flesh, smell, deep dark places where I . . .

CHARLOTTE (*shouts*). Stop it. Stop it. That's enough.

ANNE. The wound is large but shallow. It will heal.

CHARLOTTE. Take him upstairs. Remove anything from his room that might be used to cause harm and then lock the door.

EMILY. I will stay with him. He is frightened. He should not be left alone.

Lights change. Nine months later. ANNE, EMILY *and* CHARLOTTE *in the bedroom. They have just opened the post.* ANNE *and* EMILY *are reading proofs.*

EMILY. It seems that 'Wuthering' is a strange, uninviting word known to no one outside this village. They suggest 'Windy' as a better-known alternative.

ANNE. And Wildedge Hall is a real place. I suppose Wild*fell* shall do just as well.

CHARLOTTE. There has been some kind of mistake. They have sent me another cheque for a hundred pounds forgetting they have paid me already. There are more reviews. Read them and tell me if there is anything to be learned. If not, place them in the fire before I am tempted to make myself wretched again.

ANNE (*reading* CHARLOTTE*'s letter*). I enclose a cheque on account of unprecedented demand, such that a second print run will be necessary before the end of the month.

CHARLOTTE (*putting on glasses*). Let me see.

ANNE (*reading a review*). A work of genius. Utterly compelling. Flawless. Inspired. For power of expression we know not *his* equal.

CHARLOTTE (*reading*). *Jane Eyre* has been the talk of literary London. There is not a conversation to be had that does not involve its heroine. There is much curiosity about its author. Any information *he* would care to provide would be gratefully received.

ANNE (*reading*). I wish you had not sent me *Jane Eyre*. It interested me so much I have lost a whole day and half a night's work on my last chapter with the printers waiting for copy. It enthralled me utterly, some of the love passages made me cry, much to the astonishment of my servant who came in with the coals. (ANNE *turns over the page*.) . . . William Makepeace Thackeray.

CHARLOTTE *snatches the letter in disbelief.*

CHARLOTTE. Oh!

BRANWELL *enters half-dressed. He is pale and drawn. His hands tremble. The sisters hide the reviews and proofs beneath a pillow.*

BRANWELL. I have a request which will no doubt annoy but which cannot be helped on account of my purse being mislaid and not yet found. If you could see your way between you to lending me a few pence, or perhaps a full shilling. I would not ask but –

EMILY (*going to her purse*). How much do you –

ANNE. It is the third time this week. You cannot keep –

BRANWELL (*suddenly imperious*). Do not speak of me as if I were not in the room. Do not speak of me as if I were some kind of idiot. It may not be long before you shall all, all of you regret your disrespect towards your brother. I have, this very week, completed the manuscript of my novel which I will shortly be sending to the publishers. There may soon come the time when you are coming to *me* in hope of a little generosity. A little kindness.

EMILY *gives him the money. He bows and is about to leave.*

PATRICK (*entering with letter in hand*). It is a summons to court on account of debts incurred to the sum of ninety pounds.

BRANWELL. Ninety?

PATRICK. If they are not paid, the debtor will be sent to York Prison direct from the magistrate's court on Friday.

BRANWELL. It is not possible. There is some mistake.

PATRICK. That's what it says.

BRANWELL. But it was forty only a few weeks ago.

PATRICK. When debts are left unpaid they increase according to the terms on which the loan was agreed.

BRANWELL. Agreed. There was no agreement.

PATRICK. But you signed a piece of paper no doubt.

Pause.

BRANWELL (*suddenly furious*). It is robbery. *They* are the ones who should be prosecuted. Profiting by the misfortune of others. The very people who can least afford . . . (*He crumples.*) Dear God, help me. Don't let them. Don't make me. I cannot . . .

CHARLOTTE (*standing*). I have a cheque. It is money that was owed to me by my last employer.

PATRICK. Ninety pounds! How is it possible –

CHARLOTTE (*sharply*). It will pay the debt.

BRANWELL. Thank you. Bless you.

He kisses CHARLOTTE*'s hand. She remains frozen.*

It will never happen again.

Lights change. All exit except EMILY. CATHY *enters.*

CATHY. This bird was not shot. It was not. Tell me Heathcliff did not shoot it, Nelly. He promised he wouldn't. I made him promise. (*Examining the feathers.*) But there is blood. And more. Did he shoot my lapwings, did he?

August 1848. There is a pile of freshly printed copies of Wuthering Heights *and* The Tenant of Wildfell Hall *on the table. The sisters are reading reviews.*

ANNE (*reading*). *The Tenant of Wildfell Hall* contains conversations such as we had hoped never to see printed in the English language. The custom of indicating a profanity with a dash has been abandoned by Mr Bell who deems it necessary for us to read each obscenity at length.

EMILY (*reading*). Coarse and loathsome . . . vulgar in extreme . . . *Wuthering Heights* displays a morbid fascination with the grosser, animal part of our nature.

ANNE. Have you noticed that our harshest critics are all women?

EMILY (*reading*). You invite us to pity the man Heathcliff, telling us woeful tales of his orphan childhood. Do you mean us to excuse this monster who has not a drop of remorse in his body on account of his childhood beatings?

CHARLOTTE. I said myself I thought him too much the devil.

EMILY. What is the devil? How is he made? Does he drop from the womb fully formed?

CHARLOTTE (*bristling*). He is made as any man, by his own doings. By the way he chooses to live his life.

EMILY. Do you think any man would *choose* to make his own life wretched along with all around him?

CHARLOTTE. We have been given the power to think, to rise above our grievances, to choose our actions, to do what is right and good.

EMILY. Why then are we so short of compassion? So eager to condemn? We are all of us distraught at the suffering of children. We weep for their pain at the hands of monstrous adults. And yet the monstrous adults are those same children grown. If a child is crushed it doesn't grow up wise and strong and eager to assuage the sufferings of others. It longs only to be powerful. To have power over others as they did once over him. To cripple them so that they might never again do him harm. So that they might know what it is to be afraid. (*Pause.*) It is easy enough to pity something small and helpless. It takes more imagination, more courage to pity someone who frightens us.

EMILY *tears up the review and throws it on the fire.*

We are all of us monstrous in our thoughts and feelings. That we pretend to be otherwise is hardly a claim to nobility.

CHARLOTTE. Are you accusing me?

EMILY (*directly to* CHARLOTTE). Do we not revile most the things we see in others that we seek to hide in ourselves?

Pause as CHARLOTTE *strugggles to contain her rage.*

CHARLOTTE. It seems that a rumour is rife that the authors of *Wuthering Heights*, *The Tenant of Wildfell Hall* and *Jane Eyre* are one and the same person. Your publisher has sought to encourage the misapprehension in hope of increasing your sales.

Pause.

EMILY. What shall we do?

CHARLOTTE. Prove them wrong.

ANNE. How?

CHARLOTTE. The only way we can. Go to London.

EMILY. No.

CHARLOTTE. How else? I will not have them think that I
   wrote that . . .

EMILY. What?

Pause.

CHARLOTTE. Although I admire the execution, I consider the
   subjects . . . ill-chosen.

Silence.

EMILY. Anne will go. Say that your brother Ellis Bell is
   unable to come. On no account will you let it be known that
   I am a woman.

ANNE. What will we tell Father?

CHARLOTTE. The truth. He must know soon enough. There
   are copies of *Jane Eyre* in the library.

ANNE. And Branwell?

EMILY. If he asks . . . You are going to Halifax for provisions.

CHARLOTTE. Right. I will give Father *Jane Eyre* to read first
   thing tomorrow morning.

Lights change. The sound of a small handbell ringing.

ROCHESTER. It is warm. Open the window a little, and . . .
   fetch a glass of cold water.

CHARLOTTE (*as* JANE). Very well, Mr Rochester.

ROCHESTER (*startled*). Who is this? Answer me. Speak
   again.

CHARLOTTE (*as* JANE). Should it please you, sir, to sit
   closer to the window where you might feel the breeze?

   ROCHESTER *reaches for* JANE *but does not touch her.*

ROCHESTER. Jane?

CHARLOTTE (*as* JANE). Yes, sir.

ROCHESTER. What delusion, what sweet madness is this?

CHARLOTTE (*as* JANE). No delusion. No madness. It is I,
   sir.

ROCHESTER (*reaching out wildly*). Whatever, whoever you are, let me touch you or I cannot live. (*She gives him her hand.*) Her very fingers. Her wrist. Her arm. But it cannot be.

CHARLOTTE (*as* JANE). But it is.

He takes hold of her, bit by bit, and pulls her to him.

ROCHESTER. It is you, is it, Jane?

CHARLOTTE (*as* JANE). I came back to you, sir.

ROCHESTER. You are not dead in some ditch or under some stream?

CHARLOTTE (*as* JANE). I am here.

ROCHESTER. You are here? And will you stay with me?

CHARLOTTE (*as* JANE). I will.

ROCHESTER. And never leave me?

CHARLOTTE (*as* JANE). Never.

ROCHESTER. Oh sweet angel.

CHARLOTTE (*as* JANE). I will be your eyes and your hands. Your nurse, your companion –

ROCHESTER. But Jane . . .

CHARLOTTE (*as* JANE). Yes, sir.

ROCHESTER (*pulling away from her*). I want a wife.

CHARLOTTE (*as* JANE). Then you must ask for one.

ROCHESTER (*angry*). Jane, you are young. I am old and sightless. A poor blind man you must lead by the hand. Look how God has punished me for my pride. See how I am chastened.

CHARLOTTE (*as* JANE). What of it, sir?

ROCHESTER. Jane, am I not hideous to you?

CHARLOTTE (*as* JANE). No, sir. To tell the truth, sir, I love you better than before.

Lights change as we hear ANNE *calling to* PATRICK *from offstage.* PATRICK *puts on his jacket.* ANNE *enters. They are about to leave for London.* PATRICK *is visibly moved by the final scene of* Jane Eyre.

ANNE. Father, we have come to say goodbye. The gig is here and waiting.

EMILY (*entering*). It is packed and ready.

CHARLOTTE. We must go.

PATRICK. God bless you and keep you.

ANNE *and* EMILY *leave.* CHARLOTTE *pauses in the doorway. She sees the book in his hand.*

CHARLOTTE. You read it?

PATRICK. I did.

CHARLOTTE. What did you think?

Pause.

PATRICK (*takes hold of* CHARLOTTE*'s hand*). Better. Better than I expected. (*He shoos her away with his hand, afraid he will cry.*)

BERTHA *dances around* CHARLOTTE, *twirling and twirling with delight.*

Lights change. ANNE *and* CHARLOTTE *have just returned from London. They are mid-conversation, full of excitement.*

CHARLOTTE. I walked straight into his office and placed a letter he had sent me into his hand. He stared at it a moment and then at us.

ANNE. Still we said nothing.

CHARLOTTE. Then he said, 'How came you by this?' So I said, 'You sent it to me.' It took still a moment for him to comprehend –

ANNE. He stared at our crumpled skirts, our muddy shoes, our shabby case.

CHARLOTTE. When, at last, he understood, he became quite flustered with excitement. He had people he claimed would fall over themselves to meet us. Famous men who would drop everything and come running.

ANNE. Imagine our alarm.

CHARLOTTE. He wanted to arrange a party at once.

ANNE. We had to insist at length we had no desire to lose our anonymity. That our aliases would remain to all but our publishers. That we would be catching the next train back to Leeds.

CHARLOTTE. He would not be dissuaded though from booking a hotel for the weekend and taking us to the opera that night. You never saw such a place in all your life. It is hardly to be believed that human hands could create such as it is. Every inch mirrored and jewelled and –

ANNE. Picture us in our plain country garments amidst such –

CHARLOTTE. Yesterday we went to the National Gallery to see Turner's oil paintings –

ANNE. It is hard to believe it is only paint on canvas. That you could not step through the frame and feel the light on your –

CHARLOTTE. Last night we were at dinner with Mr Thackeray.

ANNE. We sat together at the end of the table, silent, too nervous to eat. He was told we were relatives visiting from the country, little accustomed to society.

CHARLOTTE. The conversation was quite unlike any I have heard before. Brilliant and yet there was a satirical turn to every phrase that made it impossible to tell if he were serious or no. He is large, ungainly, not at all handsome, and yet he was quite at home holding forth with all eyes upon him.

ANNE. At the end of the evening he came to wish us goodnight.

CHARLOTTE. I had such an attack of nerves I could neither smile nor speak and managed only to nod my head repeatedly. What is that curious affliction that renders us women dumb when we would most want to be ourselves? Afterwards I thought of a hundred things I wished I had said but as he stood there, I wanted only to hide under the table like a child.

ANNE. People are so alarming. You must think of something to say to them. And silence is so awkward. Why is that?

EMILY. We are afraid of one another. While we are talking we can pretend it is otherwise.

CHARLOTTE. All my life I have longed to see that magnificent city. To be part of that great tumult of life. And yet it was strange to be so much amongst people. To be looked at all day. By the end of the evening my head ached, my nerves raced, I never before felt such gratitude to get to my bed and the darkness. Then, only then could I think my own thoughts.

ANNE. It will take a long time for women to live in the world unafraid of its scrutiny. Neither having to make themselves a spectacle to be admired nor hiding under a bonnet. Perhaps that is why we write. That we might in silence form our thoughts, in darkness speak.

EMILY. We write to lose ourselves. To forget our sex, our shape, our name. To live other lives. To exist not as man or woman, or beauty or beast, or young or old, but to find, to find inside ourselves all manner of things . . . whole worlds, we cannot, we should not explain.

ANNE. I wish you could have seen the look on his face as he realised that we are three sisters. I never saw such a –

EMILY (*appalled*). Three?

Pause.

CHARLOTTE. He made the assumption. I thought it dishonest to refute the truth.

EMILY. But you promised.

CHARLOTTE. It would have been a lie.

EMILY. When I agreed to publish. It was a condition. You swore upon your life.

CHARLOTTE. What difference does it make? If two are sisters, why not three? It's only our publishers –

EMILY. It was not your right to disclose it.

CHARLOTTE. My right. It is not my right to speak the truth. To defend myself against –

ANNE. You are exhausted and hungry. Let us eat and talk no more until we are – rested.

CHARLOTTE. It is not my right to defend myself against allegations of obscenity, of blasphemy, of grossness and vulgarity –

ANNE. You will think differently once you're rested. Let us eat and –

CHARLOTTE. Why, why? Why will I think differently? Why must I apologise for wishing to protect my reputation? Why must I stand by and watch everything I have worked for destroyed because I am bound to some childish promise? Some absurd pact.

EMILY *stands staring at* CHARLOTTE.

A beat.

I will write tomorrow. I will let it be understood that no one, not anyone, ever will refer to Ellis Bell as a woman again. That if they fail to comply with my wishes I will terminate my contract.

BRANWELL *is heard praying.*

ANNE. What is it?

EMILY. Father is with him. He was brought home yesterday exhausted, struggling for breath. We have sent for the doctor.

CHARLOTTE. He is praying.

The prayer continues into darkness. Late evening. The sisters sit in the kitchen, exhausted. BRANWELL *is dead.* CHARLOTTE *stands.*

(*Weary.*) We must go for the undertaker.

ANNE. Now?

CHARLOTTE. It must be registered. We will need a certificate.
We must cut some hair for the mourning jewellery and
choose clothes for him to –

ANNE. It can wait 'til tomorrow.

CHARLOTTE. We should send for them to dress the body. It
is a warm night and will not be long before . . .

EMILY. We can go in the morning.

ANNE. Be still. It's over.

CHARLOTTE *weeps.*

CHARLOTTE. I do not cry for my own loss for that was long
since, but for the wreck of talent, the ruin of promise, the
dreary extinction of what might have been.

BRANWELL *returns as a child and leaps onto the table.*

BRANWELL. After one hundred days on the open seas they
catch their first sight of land. He stands at the helm and
shouts to his men. Ahoy.

ANNE. All the years it took for him to grow, to become.

BRANWELL. Land ahoy.

ANNE. It is hard to believe it. Is he really gone? He looks so
much as if he were sleeping.

BRANWELL. They see before them the mighty rocks where
the waves crash and splinter.

BRANWELL *pretends to be shot and falls to the ground.*

EMILY. The shadow spreads across his skin like a bruise. The
flush of life will not last. Even as Father holds him, he
stiffens in his arms.

BRANWELL (*pretending to drink from a bottle*). But he is
brought back to life by a magic potion.

BRANWELL *exits.*

EMILY. There is no stranger thing on this earth than to watch
the life depart and leave the body empty . . . (*Suddenly
desperate.*) What are we? Where do we go?

CHARLOTTE. We must comfort ourselves that he prayed and asked for forgiveness and spoke amen.

EMILY *goes to get her coat. She pulls it on.*

Not now. Not tonight.

EMILY *goes to the door.*

You're exhausted. You haven't eaten all day.

EMILY *picks up a loaf of bread from the table and tears off a chunk.*

Your shawl is still damp from last night. Your shoes are worn through. Your skirts are filthy.

EMILY. What of it?

CHARLOTTE. Where do you go? What do you do? What on earth do you do, hour after hour, out there alone in the darkness?

EMILY. I walk.

CHARLOTTE. Where to?

EMILY. It doesn't matter.

CHARLOTTE. Tell me.

EMILY. Anywhere. Everywhere. Just so long as I am moving. It makes me . . . calmer.

EMILY *is about to leave when a knock is heard at the back door.* BELL NICHOLLS *enters. He removes his hat.* EMILY *leaves.*

BELL NICHOLLS. I heard just now from the doctor. I came to ask if I might be of service in any way.

CHARLOTTE. No. No thank you.

BELL NICHOLLS. If there is anything at all, please do not hesitate . . . It can be a very difficult . . . a very trying –

CHARLOTTE. I said no . . . Please, Mr Nicholls, we would like to be alone.

BELL NICHOLLS. Of course, of course. Forgive me. I'm sorry. I . . .

He bows and leaves.

CHARLOTTE (*furious*). What is the matter with that ridiculous man that he must blunder in on every occasion? There is scarcely a day goes by that he does not find some excuse to –

The door reopens. BELL NICHOLLS reaches for his scarf, left on the chair.

BELL NICHOLLS. My scarf. I left it on the . . . Goodnight. (*He leaves.*)

Lights change. CHARLOTTE sits at the kitchen table trying to write. ANNE enters with a pair of BRANWELL's shoes and a box of wooden soldiers. She wraps the shoes in newspaper.

ANNE. They are hardly worn and can be sold. The clothes I shall take to the weaver's widow. The eldest boy is working now at the mill. He spends every waking hour making cloth but has barely a shirt to his name. The soldiers can go to the youngest. I doubt he will know what to do with them. He hasn't a toy in the world but a stick and pebble. That is the last. I have put his watch on Father's dressing table. He must have pawned everything else.

ANNE *looks over CHARLOTTE's shoulder.*

How is it?

CHARLOTTE. They say that success makes you bold but it is not so. I have spent all month trying to begin but it were as if twenty critics sat at my elbow and shook their heads at every sentence.

ANNE (*going to get a shoe brush*). Send a letter to your publisher. Tell him that in the light of recent events you have decided to renounce your ambitions. You intend to throw your pen into the fire and your ink down the grate. Henceforth you will lead a life of honest hard work and practicality, never more tempted by the demons to write.

CHARLOTTE. Half of my advance was spent on the funeral, the other half owed in debts.

ANNE. I'm sorry. I –

CHARLOTTE. Where's Emily?

ANNE. Fetching coal.

CHARLOTTE. She should not be so much out of doors. She stood at the graveside too long in the rain. She refused breakfast again and ate little more than a bite for dinner. These last weeks. Since . . . she has hardly spoken to me. Nor is she writing. Her pen sits untouched.

ANNE. Do you ever wonder what our lives would have been had we never put pen to paper? Had we never been afflicted by that curious condition which must have you turn life into words. Yesterday, coming back from Keighley through the wood, I was looking at the trees, at the autumn light, and trying to describe it, for it is autumn in my story, when I came upon the blackberry-pickers. They sang as they worked. There's not a soul amongst them can read or write and yet I thought I would give anything to be one of them, to be part of that great thrum of life and activity. To see the fruit of your labours in front of you at the end of the day and to know that it will be of use to others. They stopped when they saw me watching. They took off their hats and nodded and I knew that they wanted me gone. It was not a performance. The singing was not for me or anyone else. It was for its own sake. Like breathing, they did it without knowing. They didn't need anyone to hear. (*Pause.*) Why do we need someone to hear us? Why is it not enough to *be*?

CHARLOTTE. It is too late to ask. If it is an illness to write, we are already sick beyond cure.

ANNE. Why do we do it?

CHARLOTTE. Because we have to.

ANNE. But why us? Why always? As far back as I remember.

CHARLOTTE. I don't know . . . Maybe it is only compensation for having lived so very little. But I do know, when it works . . . there is no place on this earth I would rather be.

ANNE. I used to think we could change things. That by telling the truth we would make a better world.

CHARLOTTE. Maybe we will.

ANNE. There are people living in poverty, terrible injustice and suffering and we . . . we write.

CHARLOTTE. It isn't a choice. I didn't choose –

ANNE. What do we want? What is it for?

Beat.

CHARLOTTE. To have something of yourself exist . . . outside of you.

Silence.

Did you manage to describe the woods?

ANNE. Not well enough. You never saw anything so beautiful . . . and yet another week and the leaves will be gone.

EMILY *enters through the back door, dragging coal. She coughs, staggering a little.* CHARLOTTE *goes to take the coals.* EMILY *pushes her away.*

EMILY. Leave me be.

EMILY *continues. She completes her journey and begins to put coals into the fire.*

CHARLOTTE. Tomorrow we will contact the doctor.

EMILY. No.

CHARLOTTE. You are unwell. You should be in bed. You need to be –

EMILY. If you send for him I will not see him.

ANNE. Let me go to him with a list of your symptoms and get some medicine.

EMILY (*gentler*). If you must.

CHARLOTTE. He needs to *see* her. It is pointless for us to go.

EMILY (*sharply*). No. I told you. I do not wish it.

EMILY *pushes* CHARLOTTE *away as she tries to help.*

CHARLOTTE (*suddenly*). Why will you allow me to do nothing for you? Why must I always be pushed away? Why can I not love you? What is it in me? What's wrong with me?

EMILY. You want . . . too much.

CHARLOTTE. What?

EMILY. Too much of me.

EMILY *leaves, slowly meeting* CATHY. *During the following dialogue* CATHY *lies on the floor.* EMILY *lies with her head on* CATHY*'s chest.*

ANNE *and* CHARLOTTE *are still in the kitchen.*

ANNE. I think she wants to . . .

CHARLOTTE. What?

ANNE. To go.

CHARLOTTE. Go?

ANNE. I think that's what she wants.

CHARLOTTE. Go where?

ANNE. Away.

CHARLOTTE. I don't understand.

ANNE. From us.

CHARLOTTE. Go? She never went anywhere in her life. She couldn't. She wouldn't. She doesn't know how to. She –

ANNE. I mean . . . from *all* of us.

CHARLOTTE. What do you –

ANNE. From this. She has let the hawk go. When it returned she would not feed it or let it come to her. Yesterday . . . it flew away.

CHARLOTTE (*suddenly fierce*). Don't say so. Don't say so.

EMILY *is fighting for breath.* CATHY *speaks in broken sentences.* CHARLOTTE *stands at the bedroom window, looking out.*

CATHY. I am tired, tired of being. Weary to escape, to be gone, to that higher, to be always there, not seeing it dimly but with it and in it and, soon, so soon I shall be beyond –

CHARLOTTE. Don't leave me. You mustn't leave me.

CATHY. Tired, so tired of being –

CHARLOTTE. I have always known. Always, since I first saw . . . first read –

CATHY. Soon, soon I shall be –

CHARLOTTE. When I first read your poems I felt . . . I knew . . . I knew that this touched deep, went beyond. That these strange savage prayers were of a kind . . . unknown to me. That words had been made to hold all that is, that was, that *could* be. That could be were we not, were we not as we are. And I felt a sickness, a burning shame, because I knew, I knew that my own attempts to fly had been . . . as nothing. Everything I had ever written was an imitation. A poor copy. Like a bird that thinks its cage the universe, I was trapped, tethered, bound. But you, you have flown and I have watched you and in watching come to know, to know what it might be . . . to fly. For *that* I have loved and loathed you but you have been the nearest thing to my heart in all this world.

EMILY *dies.*

Did you hear me? Can you hear me?

CHARLOTTE *shakes* EMILY. *She cries out.*

No.

PATRICK *and* ANNE *kneel beside the body to pray.* ANNE *weeps.*

EMILY *and then* CATHY *rise slowly and exit in opposite directions.*

CHARLOTTE *goes to* EMILY*'s writing desk and pulls out the contents, opening bundles of paper. She is searching for something.* CATHY *speaks fragments of the poems as they are read.*

CHARLOTTE. I am happiest when most away . . .

CATHY (*leaving*). . . . happiest when most away . . . bear my soul from its home of clay . . . when I am not and none . . . nor earth nor sea nor . . . only spirit wandering wide through infinite immensity.

CHARLOTTE *finds the manuscript of* EMILY*'s unfinished novel.*

ANNE. It is almost certain that at the time of Emily's death there existed a second novel.

CHARLOTTE *sets fire to the manuscript page by page, reading each page before it burns.*

We cannot, will never know what was written on those pages. We can only guess how they came to be lost.

Perhaps in death, Emily could be hers, to protect, to possess, as she had never been in life.

Lights change. ANNE *and* CHARLOTTE *are in the middle of an argument.*

CHARLOTTE. The seaside! You can scarcely climb the stairs.

ANNE. The air is cleaner. The seawater a natural tonic. It has been known to cure all manner of ills.

CHARLOTTE. Perhaps when you're stronger. We will wait until –

ANNE. It will not wait. If we wait it may be too . . . (*Pause. She struggles to find the words.*) I cannot express it but I have a desire, a longing to see once more the ocean. To hear that . . . mighty roar and tumult. To hear that ceaseless shifting, that endless . . . song. To feel myself lost in it. To know that it *was* before and will be . . . will be still. Forgive me but I have often, too often doubted, have questioned a God that can allow such misery, such suffering and injustice –

CHARLOTTE. Don't tell me.

ANNE. I feel . . . that is, I *hope* that such a sight will cure me of this doubt . . . this despair.

CHARLOTTE. We will go.

CHARLOTTE *and* ANNE *walk forward together. Huge sound of waves crashing onto the shingle. The sun is setting.*

ANNE *leans upon* CHARLOTTE. *The sound reaches a crescendo then cuts out.* ANNE *walks towards the back wall slowly.* CHARLOTTE *stands alone, holding* ANNE*'s shawl and writing folder. She takes it to the table and reads, as we hear* ANNE *speaking.*

ANNE.
A dreadful darkness closes in
On my bewildered mind.

Not only for the past I grieve
The future fills me with dismay.

Another page.

I looked around in wild despair
I called him but he was not there
Oh Lord, hear a wretch's prayer.

CHARLOTTE.
I looked around in wild despair
I called him but he was not there
Oh Lord, hear a wretch's prayer.

CHARLOTTE *is crying while scoring out lines of poetry, replacing them with her own amendments.* CHARLOTTE*'s rewriting is an attempt to bear the unbearable. To reinvent her sisters in her memory as calmer, more devout, less complex beings.*

EMILY. When Charlotte published a new volume of collected poetry later that year, virtually every one of her sister's poems was altered. Some were small changes. A word. A line. But others were unrecognisable.

Lights change. Six months later.

CHARLOTTE. In the daytime, occupation comes to my aid, but when evening closes and night approaches – the house is silent. The rooms empty. I long for sleep but I dream of them, not in health, but as they were in sickness and suffering. I have been twice to London this year, hoping to escape, but it little suited my purpose. I have become a celebrity. Everywhere I go I am looked at and talked about. I will ever more be a curiosity, the author of *Jane Eyre.*

There is currently a stage version which I declined to see in spite of much entreaty. I was instead taken to see Macready in *Macbeth*. What a strange thing the theatre is. I astounded a dinner party by saying I thought him mannered and artificial. I produced a blank silence, at the end of which the hostess changed the subject. The outcome of all this attention was two days of continuous headache on my return. The silence here is unbearable. How diminished are life's adventures when you have lost those who would share our tribulations, our insights, our delights.

After 'the silence here is unbearable', BRANWELL, ANNE and EMILY cross through the space and exit.
CHARLOTTE finishes speaking and crosses to the stairs, pausing as she feels EMILY's ghost pass her shoulder.

Lights change. PATRICK enters.

PATRICK. There is something I need to tell you. It will no doubt surprise you as it did myself. You have received a proposal of marriage. I told him that you have no intention of marrying and though he seems at present somewhat cast down by the news it will, no doubt, pass. This morning he handed in his resignation so it will not be long before his departure.

CHARLOTTE. Resignation.

PATRICK. It will be a little awkward for a day or two but he will be gone soon enough.

CHARLOTTE. Who is it?

PATRICK. Mr Bell Nicholls.

CHARLOTTE (*astonished*). Mr Bell Nicholls.

PATRICK. He tells me he has loved you for some years. That he meant to propose to you some time ago but that the tragic events of these last months deemed it unfitting so he does so now.

CHARLOTTE. Mr Nicholls.

PATRICK. I told him there was no prospect. None at all. That I considered it an impertinence that he should entertain such a notion. That he was quite deluded to imagine himself a fitting suitor to a woman of your standing. Your achievements. He has, as I said, given his notice so you need not fear for further embarrassment. The matter is quite closed. Let us speak of it no more.

BERTHA *rolls and stretches on the floor joyously.*

Lights change. Three months later. CHARLOTTE *alone in the kitchen writing. A knock at the door.* CHARLOTTE *opens it to* ARTHUR BELL NICHOLLS. *He has a book in hand and looks extremely embarrassed.*

BELL NICHOLLS. Forgive me for calling uninvited. I hope you received my letter. I wrote to say that I might . . . that I would be passing through the parish on Christmas Eve, that is today, and thought to return a book which I took by mistake, having borrowed it from your father some time ago and forgotten to –

CHARLOTTE. The answer is 'yes'.

BELL NICHOLLS. I'm sorry?

CHARLOTTE. To your question.

BELL NICHOLLS. I'm not sure I –

CHARLOTTE. My father was mistaken in his assumption.

BELL NICHOLLS. You mean –

CHARLOTTE. I will give him the book.

BELL NICHOLLS. Yes . . . Thank you.

CHARLOTTE. And I will tell him that I wish to be married. It may take some time to persuade him. We will have to be patient.

BELL NICHOLLS. Indeed.

CHARLOTTE. I shall have unexceptional expectations. I am not young or beautiful and have long since grown out of fantasies of a perfect union –

BELL NICHOLLS. Of course.

CHARLOTTE. I realise there is much to be sacrificed. I shall endeavour to make a good wife. I do not, as you know . . . love you, but it will be my hope that through perseverance and attention to duty, my feelings will . . . in the fullness of time . . . ripen towards –

BELL NICHOLLS (*embarrassed*). Yes. Yes. Indeed.

CHARLOTTE. Very well.

BELL NICHOLLS. I am overcome with gratitude and yet I scarcely believe my ears. You have not answered my letters, not one, nor sought any kind of contact since –

CHARLOTTE. My life at present is spent too much alone. Much as I value my writing, it has come, perhaps, at the expense of other things. A life lived, not in the head, but in the real world, such as it is.

BELL NICHOLLS (*overcome*). You are certain. You will not come to regret your –

CHARLOTTE. All my life I have longed to be admired, to be revered for some extraordinary achievement. And yet the more I live, the more I come to suspect that happiness is not to be found in the praise, the adulation of strangers. That in fact this need to be special, to be exceptional may be the very cause of one's loneliness, setting you apart as it does. That it is in our ordinariness, in our imperfection, in the detail of life, that contentment is found. At least I am hoping so.

BELL NICHOLLS. Thank you. Thank you.

CHARLOTTE. Your letters. They moved me. I had not expected to ever inspire such . . . such –

BELL NICHOLLS. Forgive me.

CHARLOTTE. I will give Father the book.

Lights change. CHARLOTTE *is writing at the table.* BELL NICHOLLS *hangs up his coat and comes to read over her shoulder.*

My dear friend. Since I came home from honeymoon I have not had an unemployed moment. My life is changed indeed. I have no time for thinking. His bent is so much towards matters of real life and usefulness, so little inclined to the contemplative. He has just now returned from a meeting of the weavers who hope to form some kind of union. He has great hopes but will not say so. My husband is not a poet or a poetical man and yet I am happy.

Arthur has just glanced over my shoulder. He thinks I have written too freely and says you must promise to burn my letter. You must comply or in future you shall receive such letters as he writes to all save myself. Plain statements of fact without so much as a single flourish. If a phrase of affection steals in, it does so on tiptoe, blushing.

My health has been very good since my honeymoon until about ten days ago indigestion and continual faint sickness have been my portion.

EMILY. Charlotte died just nine months after her marriage. Three weeks before her thirty-ninth birthday.

ANNE. She was pregnant and suffering from an acute form of morning sickness. A condition that might easily be cured today.

EMILY *and* ANNE *are beginning to unbutton their Victorian clothes.* CHARLOTTE *reads from the biography.*

CHARLOTTE. To speak truth, my sufferings are very great. My nights indescribable. Sickness and pain with scarce a reprieve. My husband is the tenderest nurse, the kindest support, the best earthly companion that woman ever had. His patience never fails and is tried by sad days and broken nights. My heart is knit to him entirely.

All exit as CATHY *enters with pillow, talking. She climbs up onto the table.*

CATHY. Wheeling over our heads in the middle of the moor. Riding the wind, higher and higher. Making us run.

She throws handfuls of feathers into the air.

Fly. Fly. Fly away from here. You must be gone. Away. Away. Away now quickly before they catch you.

Blackout.

End.